The Church, The Gospel and Society

by

P. T. FORSYTH, M.A., D.D.

WIPF & STOCK · Eugene, Oregon

Wipf and Stock Publishers
199 W 8th Ave, Suite 3
Eugene, OR 97401

The Church, The Gospel and Society
By Forsyth, P. T.
ISBN 13: 978-60899-170-9
Publication date 11/17/2009
Previously published by Independent Press, 1962

FOREWORD

THIS book is a reprint of the two addresses given by my father in 1905, in London and Leeds respectively, in his capacity as Chairman of the Congregational Union of England and Wales. The fact that they were originally spoken from a pulpit, and not specially prepared for a printer, does affect their style. They were first produced, immediately after they were spoken, as threepenny pamphlets, and they have never before appeared in book form; but they have been so emphatically asked for, the pamphlets being all but non-existent, that the publishers feel justified in re-issuing them as a book.

As happened in the case of other reprints of my father's books, the question arose as to allusions which are today out-of-date—should they be deleted or retained? I have followed the same principle which was recommended to me then by the theologians and ministers whom I consulted (some of whom had been trained by him), namely, that passing references which may now seem anachronisms do not detract in any way from the value for today of the great thesis of both addresses. Later readers have indeed suggested that the political allusions (e.g. to the House of Lords, and to the vital connexion between Congregationalism and Liberalism in 1905) form a valuable piece of social history.

JESSIE FORSYTH ANDREWS.

A HOLY CHURCH THE MORAL GUIDE OF SOCIETY

I DESIRE to write of a holy Church as the moral guide of society. By a holy Church I mean a Church holy in its calling rather than its attainment either in work or truth. I do not allude to the Church as an authority, but as the apostle and agent of the authority. It is not the light, but the candlestick. It is not the word, but the witness. The authority is the word of grace committed to the Church in trust. Therefore, I do not think of the Church as the moral example, but as Christ's executor, as the trustee of the moral principle of Redemption. This principle it has to apply as a standard to certain practices of society; but it has also to do much more. It has to infuse it into the very structure of society as its organizing principle.

What I venture to say falls into two heads—the matter of principle and the matter of practice.

I. THE PRINCIPLE OF THE MATTER

The great problem before civilization is the moral problem. Our crisis is intellectual, no doubt, but it is still more ethical. We spend our strength upon many false issues, upon many trivial and ritual issues, with the result that if even we reach the really great ones, we are apt to do so either jaded or untrained. We therefore shrink from facing them. Our prominent preachers never seem to face final questions. Audiences do not welcome them, and the press evades them. But they face us. They will not be evaded. And among them the moral problem is the problem of the hour and of the future. For it is the whole social problem. It is the issue on which civilization depends for its permanence; and yet it is the problem which civilization alone is least able to solve. But it is the problem on whose solution Christianity stands or falls. A Christianity which is out of relation to it is a false Christianity, however pious it may be; it is unscriptural, however biblical; it is hollow, however popular; and it is inhuman, in fact, however sympathetic it may sound in tone.

We are a great body of Free Churchmen, and I have long been impressed with the fact that the Free Churches have been gaining more in public attention than in public weight. They are forces more than guides. Their bulk tends to outgrow their influence. That is easy if they relax their gospel, or if they apply it but to the cry of the hour, and become a branch of journalism, or the prey of the press. I cannot avoid certain misgivings. Do they realize the moral situation on the large scale? Has the question of the spiritual authority even faintly dawned on them? Have they quite grasped the great social problem which they certainly feel? Is their idea of the Church problem ample enough? Is their interest in the evangelical problem always on sound lines? Do they keep their footing on the *moral* centre of Christianity—on the work of Christ? Has the note of the Church as free impaired its higher note as holy? Will you forgive me for frankly stating these questions?

I

The great public question, after all, is, How are we to think of Christian love? It is a question that must seem very grotesque to the *Daily Mail* and its tribe. But how grotesque the tribe is to the sacred irony that sits in heaven and laughs, watching the puny politics of the hour, and weaving them into the mighty strategy of the race and the Kingdom. Yet there is a conception of Christian love which may well seem ineffective to the man of affairs and of history. If love meant but pity it would be a feeble factor in the great course of the world. If it meant mere friendliness, or mere affection, there is nothing in its charm that would justify our faith in its final triumph. If it meant but philanthropy, and if the final judgment turned wholly on our life's obedience to precepts of brotherly kindness or non-resistance, then love would not give us a basis for political action on the large scale. It has not enough of ethical principle in it. It is too small and personal in its dimensions. Whatever may be its relation to certain timely *precepts*, or even parables, of Christ, like that of the judgment in Matthew xxv., it does not cover the whole field of Christian love as revealed in His Gospel. We are not judged by our Christian kindness alone, but by our Christian faith. No single parable or precept covers the whole Gospel. No single one rises to the dimensions of the Fatherhood revealed in the cross, and felt from there. The father of the prodigal is not so great and holy as the Father of our Lord Jesus Christ crucified. There is a conception vaster and more public than the prodigal's father, no less full of glow and still more full of grace. Redemption is a greater thing than forgiveness, and the prodigal's father did not redeem. Love stands before us in its whole gospel fullness as a world-principle and power no less than a gracious affection. For great public purposes of Church or State the principle of moral holiness in the Atonement is of far more value than the dear affection of the heart, more precious than the pity even of Christ, taken alone, and more effective than the teaching of Christ. You are not certain of that? Return and ask the great Christian through whom, more than any other, Christianity has become a power in modern democracy, who, through his Puritans, has made our Free Churches, and who is also one of the greatest and soundest commentators as to the teaching of Scripture. I mean Calvin.

That was a man who knew his gospel and knew his world. We cannot accept all his doctrines, especially his negations, but we have much to learn to-day from his principles. He it was who seized and developed that side of the Gospel which engrosses us to-day—the social side—in a way the German reformers never did. And whatever errors he committed there were two of ours he escaped. He did not pursue his great and lasting social effects by merely sympathetic means. That is a misuse of sympathy; it is sentimentalism. And in using moral means he did not look for his principle in the precepts of Christ, but in the cross of Christ. For public and social purposes God's love means more than sympathy. Sympathy is not adequate to redeem. God's love is all sympathy, and more. It is sanctity. It means the moral principle of holiness which in the cross is in standing conflict with the egoism which rules the world.

It is the frame of holy mind which is engrossed with the righteous weal of others, whether the heart melt, or thought toil, or the will move. It is the true social principle—as spontaneous as passion, itself a passion, and yet safe from passion's tides; as kind as pity, but far more wise; as intense as affection, and no less full of devoted service and sacrifice. This is what corresponds to the love of 1 Cor. xiii., or 1 John. It is in this way that we are to love Christ more than parent, wife, or child—with another, yet not alien, love, with a love which is greater in kind rather than degree. It is creating rather than created love. It is a real social and political principle, wider than man and kinder than woman. It moves us both to private concern for souls, and to a general concern for the State and for the race. It combines the near kindness and the far. It unites close love with long wisdom. It is preoccupied with its own duties and others' rights no less than their needs. It delivers politics from the taint of charity by the grace of charity, by the just, yea, holy charity of grace. Politics ceases, then, to be a partial system of doles, and legislation a mere series of passing reliefs. This holy love enlarges charity to the dimensions of justice, and confirms mercy with the assurance of righteousness and peace. It finds in progressive law and order one of the great charities of God to human need. And upon that gift it puts a grace. It sets up a kingdom rooted in the infinite moral holiness of a redeeming God. God's love has given us a settled and political society. Then surely both the care and the conversion of that social order is a true service of God, and a true work of the love which is holy, and not merely kind. Christian holy love may take the form of benevolence on the one hand, or of conciliation on the other, but it must also for public purposes take the form of righteousness. And there is great scope for Christian wisdom in deciding which form it should take in particular cases. But it is quite certain that Christ's treatment of the public authorities did not carry out His precept of non-resistance, or of giving upon demand—say the demand for a sign.

There is not a constitution nor a polity in the world that does not lend itself but too readily to the schemes of egoism. Imperialism and Socialism are in this alike. There is not an institution that does not need constant vigilance as the price of its freedom and blessing. And it is difficult for most men not to make public facilities subserve their private interest. In these circumstances it is a mighty public matter that there should reign in the soul a principle, with the force of a passion and the authority of a religion, to consider first the common weal in the faith of a common salvation through holy love. Nothing less than religion can bring about such a result. In this sense love of the brotherhood is a powerful political principle; and in this great sense nothing but Christianity can bring brotherhood to pass. If it do not bring it to pass it is not Christianity, and the Church is no true Church. The Church of an interest, or party, or nation is not the Church of Christ, nor its faith New Testament faith, nor its love Christ's love. The holy principle of Christian love is so comprehensive that all other ethical principles are included in it. And it is so exalted that all sectional, or national principles are by it either placed or absorbed. The extravagances of its fantastic apostles must never blind us to the essential royalty of the principle itself. For its incarnation is Christ, and its destiny is the Kingdom of Almighty Holy God.

But are we keeping our footing on the moral centre of social Christianity—on the holy work of Christ?

II

What I have to say on this head will be pervaded by four main principles which I would lay down at the outset, and then enlarge.

1 The main work of the Church is determined by the nature of the Saviour's work in the cross, and not by human demands.

(2) This work was the condensed action of His whole personality—His whole holy personality.

(3) The Saviour's work being personal was therefore ethical, and not official. But by ethical I mean that its keynote was holiness. The great need of the Church therefore is not work, but sanctity in the ethical evangelical sense.

(4) The *essence* of Christ's work was the securing once for all of the Kingdom of God in the real world unseen, by an ethical and spiritual victory. He set up a Holy Kingdom by a moral act of final judgment on the prince (or principle) of evil. The historic *scope* of this work of the Saviour was the whole of Society. And the *object* of it was the gradual conversion of actual Society into the Kingdom of God which He had already secured, the moral Kingdom befitting

a holy God. Christ was no mere individual, but "a public person." And His holiness is not a pietist but a public holiness, a social righteousness with a saintly soul.

The prime object of the Saviour was not to exhibit to us God's love, but to deal adequately for us with God's holiness, and deal with it in kind, by holiness. Christ's first concern, have you noticed, was, Hallowed be Thy name; then, Thy Kingdom come. The greater side of Christ's life was the Godward side; and it is almost wholly turned away from us. His first concern was God's; and God's first love is His own holiness, then the man He made to share it. He loved it so much that, when man failed it, He redeemed and reconciled him to it. The point of first moment in the Gospels is not the natural character of Jesus and its development, but His sonship, that which only the Father knows; it is not His interest for the modern man, but His value to Holy God.

Here there is a clear collision between modern humanism and the Gospels. Humanism is concerned with the interesting Christ, the historic character and its psychology. But in the Gospels Jesus is a historic character only in the second place. The fact may have its difficulties, but at least it puts us less at the mercy of historic criticism. In the first place He is the Son with whom the Father has a superhuman understanding unique in kind and mediatorial in function (Matt. xi. 25), in whom also the Holy Father is always well pleased. In other and modern words, He is the perfect satisfaction offered in life, and in death especially, to a holiness which nothing but holiness can satisfy or atone. He orders Himself by the Father's holy will, not by men's piteous demands; He is moved by Divine requirement, more even than by human need. It is the action of the Father for our salvation that is the first theme of the New Testament—the Father's action in the Son, first on Himself, then on us. Christ is there primarily as the moral agent of the moral act of Redemption by God—an agent so perfect and final that He was Holy

Godhead itself redeeming (2 Cor. v. 21). The humane, historic, and psychological Jesus is nothing without the theological Christ—so far as the first sources, and even the Gospels, instruct us. His first concern was with something He had to bring to God in the name of God's holiness, and His second was with what He brought men in the name of God's love. For love is but holiness in the outgoing; and it is not a moral power till holiness is behind it and above it. And holiness is moral majesty or it is nothing. So viewed the work of Christ was ethical, final, and positive. It was something which had a completeness of its own before human experience, and apart from it.

It must make a difference quite revolutionary to the action of Christianity on the world, if we think of the central act of Christ and of history as essentially an ethical act—not juridical but moral, not the pivot of a scheme, but the achievement of a person, not preliminary but final. On the other hand, it must make much difference that Christ's action is not the saving of an *élite* out of Society, but the saving of Society as a whole through an elect. And, in the third place, it must make a vast difference to the action of the Church whether it is creating a Kingdom of God as we go on, or introducing one finished and foregone, whether it is laying the track or uncovering it. How shall I be perfectly sure that something will not occur one day to upset all the Church is doing to produce the Kingdom? Only if I am sure the Kingdom is already there, mystically perfect, and waiting to come in. And as sure as death it is there—as sure as Christ's death which put it there.

The Kingdom as a reality exists outside of us since Christ finished His work of establishing it. What we have to do is not to produce it but to introduce it. It works in us mightily. It urges us on more irresistibly than the instinct of race. All we do for it is drawn from it; it does not come into being by what we do. The Christian lives on the Kingdom; the Kingdom does not live on the Christian. And how different, I say, our mien would be if we took that home; how calm, how strong, how unfevered, how effectual. There is a calm which is a mere matter of temperament, and there is a peace which is that of faith. The former is not at our command; but the latter is. And it makes a great difference in the agents of the Kingdom whether they think they are making it or bringing in what is already made; whether they regard the crises of history as knots that men must untie or as saving judgments of God and under-agents in the one decisive judgment, which is the salvation of the cross. The former may be prophets, but the latter are apostles. For the former everything is to do, for the latter all is done. The former strive and cry, the latter watch, work, pray. But why do not both think more?

These are the principles I wish first to expand, then to apply. They furnish the *only* base and commission for a social Gospel in the great sense of the word.

Our Lord did not come only to save souls, or to gather devout groups, or even to found Churches; but so to save souls and found Churches as to make Christian nations, and thus change Society to the Kingdom of God. Christianity is in its genius supernational and ultramontane. But it acts not by crushing the nations under a religious nation, political like themselves only landless, like the Roman Church. It acts by developing the nations under a king, and an obedience, moral, inward, universal, and unseen. It develops each nation because it transcends all, and gives to each its call and place. Now, the Free Churches have been political enough, but, as Dr. Mackennal used to urge, they have not been national enough in their ideas of a universal Christianity. They have not, till lately, stepped out of the idea of a private Church, bred in them by a persecution which haunts them still. They have not put out into the swelling stream of a manifold national life. But lately the larger movement has begun, especially in the Free Church Federation.

III

The Church in general begins to realize this public vocation as it has never done before. I will illustrate this first by a symptom, which is open to some remark, and then by one with which I sympathize more.

(1) We hear appeals to the Churches to realize that the Church is *primarily* a working Church. Now is this so? Is it not the extravagance of a principle sound enough in itself? It is an extravagance which disfigures and almost disqualifies an able and genial American book by Dr. Gladden on pastoral theology. The extravagance only takes another form when it is said the Church is before all else a missionary Church, whether at home or abroad. Is the Church first and foremost a working Church? Would it not be more missionary if it were more of something else first? Has the Church not something to do before it go to work on the world? Has it not first to believe? Is it not first a believing Church—the congregation of the faithful? The Church is made by faith; and has faith its old value with us? Is the Church not, next, a holy and worshipping Church, paying a tribute to the God it believes in before it is fit to pay anything to the men it would help? The hallowing of God's name precedes the coming of His Kingdom. It does so in Christ's prayer. It does so in Christ's saving work. And it should do so in our saved service. Our Churches need a spirit of holiness far more than a spirit of work, and they need it for the work's sake and the sake of love. Then is the Church not, next, a loving Church? Its faith is nothing if it do not work out into mutual love among the believing brethren, and compel attention to the way those Christians love one another. And only then is it a working Church. For what is the use of a Church setting to work among men unless we can show them, burning in ourselves, a faith and love which make our way better than theirs? The hearts of some able

and faithful ministers are well-nigh broken by the popularity of the demand that every Church to do its duty must be above all else a hive of external Christian activities. And it is cruel and worldly to put money into the Church fabric, while the minister is underpaid to constant anxiety. I have the warmest sympathy with our institutional missions. It is true that if a Church be not at work it is no Church. If it is not missionary it will cease to be a Church. But to say that the Church, as distinct from its missions, is primarily a working society is to secularize it. In some, in many, cases the agencies have become of more interest than the Communion. The work may represent an itch of activity rather than an inspiration of service. It is English restlessness rather than Christian energy. And it burns itself out.

We are unsettled and troubled about many things. And so, in our British way, we take a header into action, partly to dull misgiving, partly to indulge our instincts. But it is action too often fussy, fevered, and ill-considered. It is groping action, with a tendency to demonstration rather than deeds. May I bid you pause to note that Christ's miracles were deeds of single-hearted sympathy and service? They were not evidential, not advertisement, not ostentation. He would not allow them to be used in the way of demonstrations. His demonstration was of the Spirit and its power. But we do not proceed always with that sure, calm, spiritual command of the moral situation which was Christ's note; as it has been the great note of the Church in the ages of its creative and revolutionary action on the world.

IV

(2) But the new social concern of the Church appears in another direction. There is a new interest in the largest social questions from the moral side. There is a desire to

re-examine our social and industrial conditions in the light of Christian ethics. And the result is disquieting. The Church has been widely moved by Christian compassion, but it begins to be moved also by Christian compunction. It has an uneasy sense of something wrong, and some people guilty, in the existing order of things. There is a dim sense, right or wrong, that the relations of the Church to wealth and comfort are in collision with the teaching of Christ. The passion for property and power, for more business and more empire, is uneasy in contact with Christ's apparent renunciation of both. Christ, the morally clear, single-eyed, and self-sure Christ, seems, even to the Church, a rebuke rather than an inspiration in the confusion of the age. We used to defend Christian truth, champion orthodoxy, "do something for the Godhead of the Eternal Son." Now our truth turns round on us with a swift irony and judges us. Our palladium becomes our rebuke. From champions we become culprits (which is a much more respectful attitude on our part). Moreover, in our uneasiness we not only hit out wildly, but we are unhappy on wrong grounds—not without reason, but with reasons partly wrong. We are apt, I have already hinted, to take our chief stand upon the *precepts* of Christ. They seem very simple, and they provoke some bitterness by their contrast with our complex and sophisticated age to which we directly apply them, directly—as if 2,000 years had not come and gone, or as if we had never read a word of Church history in our lives. Would Christ say in present circumstances exactly what He said in an age so totally different as His own? Would He tell us to give to him that asketh, or forbid us to keep a balance at the bank? We make Him a legislator, as if He were a finer Moses. We are all ritualists by nature, and we think it grace. On the strength of some of these precepts of Christ, turned into injunctions for all time, we set up a new kind of social Judaism. We admire a fine legalist like Hillel, and naïvely wonder why Christ did not. And we are in danger of losing the Gospel in the Gospel's humane law. We make the cardinal mistake of thinking that the Kingdom of God was set up in the ideal precepts of Jesus, instead of in His cross. But it is by the cross we are to read all the precepts, and, if necessary, revise them. Christ's action on the world is not preceptual. Almost all the social dissatisfaction with Christianity starts from the fallacy that it is. People treat the New Testament as a Christian code. But this is entirely foreign to the genius of Christianity. It is falling from grace with Galatian levity. Precepts may be but local, temporary, individual. And they always tend to become either casuistic or out of date. Moreover, the apostles (it is very remarkable) did not appeal to standing precepts of Christ, but to His spirit. They prescribe Christian duties in a free fashion from the mind and spirit produced by grace. Christ's supreme eternal work is in His cross, which contains, along with the power, the principle which solves the problem of every age. And it yields the principle to the faith that questions it severely from a thorough knowledge of the age.

Two things we discuss much, but we do not *measure*—the old cross and the crisis of to-day. And we do not correlate them. We read the cross without knowing the context of the world it stands in. And we too often approach the world without that searching and stable sense of the final reality of Christ's cross which alone can make headway against the near and urgent orders of the day. And then, stunned by these pushing importunities, we are dull even to the subtler forces within *them*. Have we a real, relevant message to the greatest powers now ruling the world—say, to finance? The cross has. Have we? To our Churches in the gross, is the holy public Christ a reality as practical and piercing as business, family, property, law, politics, and empire? We listen and approve when we hear about the fatal attention so long given to speculative doctrine and theology. We accept the invitation to be more heartful and ethical in our interests; yes, and all the time our ethic grows thin, strident, trivial, and negligible by men of affairs. We have the ethical *note*—that is well. But have we the ethical *word*—the sound and relevant moral word, for the age? If not, why not? Because we have relaxed our piercing interest in the great ethical power-centre of the world, which is God's holy achievement once for all in the cross. Because that central and creative point has been captured first by the jurists of old, and now by the sentimentalists and mere moralists of to-day. It has been either neglected or individualized out of all public ethical authority.

V

The source of the Kingdom of God was not the teaching of Christ, which was illustrative and not constitutive. That teaching, indeed, was a failure with those to whom it was principally addressed. The Jews crucified Him in spite of it; and it is preserved to us only in manuals of instruction prepared for Churches which had been made otherwise, namely, by the gospel of the cross. Nor was the source of the Kingdom the calling of the disciples; in spite of the call and teaching they became estranged and renounced Him. It was not even the resurrection of Christ, which was but God's seal set upon a greater work already finished. It was not Pentecost, which was but the sequel and emergence of the great achievement in its social power. You agree, perhaps. The Kingdom was founded in none of these things, and certainly not in Christ's teaching. You hasten to say it was founded in His person. But I would carry you farther one step. His person was not inert. It is not a rock foundation, but a soul foundation, that carries the great Church. It rests not on a solid substance, but on a saving will. The Kingdom took rise in a new creative act. In its beginning was not the word merely, nor the thought, but the deed. The whole person of Christ was here for the moral act in which it was consummated—for the cross, the dying of the Holy One and Just. The cross is the real foundation of the Kingdom. *There* was condensed the conscience of Christ and the holiness of eternity—and *there* arose, in consequence, the ethic of human society. The Kingdom was expounded, indeed, by parables, but it was founded on the cross, and upon the holiness which made the central issue of the cross.

Remember always that the holiness of God is not a mystical idea, but a moral. It is not the luxury of goodness, but its soul. It is not the perfume, but the bath of regeneration. It is central, therefore, to the great moral organization which we call human Society. All our hope for Society rests on the spread in it of a Divine and righteous love. But holiness is the foundation of Divine love, and the bloom on Divine righteousness. What Paul from his education calls the righteousness revealed in the cross is what is elsewhere called holiness. It is the great white throne. It is the perfection of God's moral nature. It is ethic upon the whole eternal scale. It is the eternal unity of God's free will with His perfect nature. It is the supreme expression of His absolute perfection. But His *moral* perfection, observe. Holiness is not the calm balance and self-possession of an infinite of Eternal Being, as it appeared to Plotinus or Spinoza. It is more akin to the self-conquest, self-bestowal, and self-effectuation which belong to an eternal moral personality. This is the true Christian sense of holiness, as distinguished from the thought of God as the Supreme Being, inviolable, self-sufficing, and splendid. In this latter sense holiness gives us but an æsthetic religion, culminating in a future more paradisal than heavenly. It is the Catholic idea, the Dantesque.

And it is anti-social. The public condition of Catholic peoples is due to this non-ethical sense which is primary in their conception of holiness, which associates it with God's essence or aspect rather than His action, and which makes the ideal life one of contemplation and the beatific gaze rather than one of personal communion. As a consequence, grace is the sacramental infusion of a Divine substance, rather than the exercise of the holiest mercy. Whatever is the unity of a moral God must be the moral unity of Society. The unity of a tri-personal God is the foundation of unity for a society of persons. But the unity of a trinity of persons is a *moral* unity rather than a metaphysical. It is a *Holy* Trinity. And the foundation of our belief in it is (as it was for Athanasius) the holy act of redemption rather than the stately philosophy of the Logos. That is to say, in the Holy Cross we have the moral principle of the universe which the Church has to administer and adjust to the successive phases of human society.

VI

But the word principle itself may mislead us. The core of the cross is not merely the *revelation* of God as holy, but the *effectuation* of His holiness, the practical establishment of it upon its destruction of the kingdom of evil. The soul of the atonement is only negatively and individually described as the forgiveness of sin. It forgives by establishing in the world of spiritual reality the inflexible supremacy of God's ethical holiness, through an act which affects at once the whole of God and the whole of human Society. If such an one died for all, in that act all died. It therefore commits Society to a development to that holy end. The object of historic Society is now, since that act *at the creative centre of history*, the evolution of holiness, and its actual establishment as the controlling principle of human relations. Society can only cohere and prosper in a faith with an ethical core, whose inmost place is holiness, and holiness its final goal.

I seek a city, and a city which has foundations. And this holy city has two foundations—first, Christ's final satisfaction of the holiness of God; second, His final destruction of the kingdom of the unholy. They are two aspects, upwards and downwards, of His one act. They are both absolute, and both foregone. And the basis of all that I say is the necessary, the dynamic connection between Christ's satisfaction of God's holiness on the cross (with its destruction of the evil kingdom once for all) and the moral organization of society. And I urge that Christ's offering to God, while foiling the last resource of the evil Kingdom, was the actual establishment of God's Kingdom, and did not simply lead to it. The Kingdom of God is already set up, in the mystic and urgent world of reality, by the ethical and universal nature of that absolute act of holiness in the cross at the spiritual centre of history in Christ's soul. By the complete judgment *and execution* of evil, which was effected through the perfect action of holiness there, Christ has set up the Kingdom. It is now a spiritual reality, which is bound to enter and bind the strong man. It must capture the existing order, and establish itself not only amidst Society (as a separate Church), but as the new organization of Society itself. Its absolute victory must take effect in a moral reconstruction of Society. But, of course, if the first interest of the cross was not the effective vindication and establishment of God's holiness, then an ethical kingdom is not a first necessity as its result. A cross which acts first on sinful men and not on Holy God is not strong enough to organize men into a perfectly ethical society of love, or to moralize their institutions into God's Holy Kingdom.

VII

I will put it otherwise. We dream, we more than dream, of a millennium of Society, to arrive through historic and ethical growth, not through a catastrophe arresting history. But can it have any other meaning than the final victory in Society of goodness? But how is this possible without religion? Without religion, Society would be maimed of at least one of its great energies. But religion, if it have place at all, takes the ruling place. A religion worth anything to Society is the ruling power in Society. But what is a social religion without some object of faith? and, unless the positivists are right, it must be an object other than the Society it would amend and rule. For such a result its object must be a goodness established above and beyond the changes, desertions, and assaults of Society. Nay, more; the assault and sin of Society has challenged, renounced, and overthrown that goodness in human affairs. Therefore the object of the social faith we need must be more than a goodness that cannot be shaken in itself—a goodness invulnerable; it must be a goodness indefectible, which establishes itself out of the shock of human wickedness, destroys that wickedness by a central judgment, recovers all in principle, and at last covers all in fact. The object of our religious faith, in any effective social religion, must be something more than a mere revelation of absolute goodness as a rock of ages amid the storm. It must be more than a manifestation, it must be an achievement. It must be the self-establishment of this absolute goodness, that is, of holiness, by an act not of completion merely for the past, nor of inception merely for the future, but of final triumph at the moral centre of the world; an act not perfective, but redemptive. Now, a moral centre can only be a moral personality. I need not argue that here. And if so, it can be no other than Christ. The Kingdom is gathered up in the King. The King makes the Kingdom, not the Kingdom the King. And in Christ it is the cross; which is the true meeting-point of the historic and the absolute, the supreme and decisive act of Time and Eternity, of man in God and God in man. There is no moral Society possible except by a religion which turns on holiness, and whose supreme interests gather actually and not speculatively at the point where Holy God overcame the world.

If we regard the moral question as the great question, it is really a religious one. It is a question about the primacy of holiness, the ultimacy of it, for God, for Christ, for the Church, for the Soul, for Society. Especially so for the Church. Yet go over the Churches, and ask if holiness be their first practical interest and the chief impress they make on the world in contact with them. There is but one answer: It is not so. Their holy cross is not in moral command of social conduct and relations. And the cause? The chief cause is a misconstruction of the cross. Either salvage has ousted salvation, and the cross has been treated as a mere life-saving apparatus for personal escape; or it has been made the servant of human needs instead of the agent of God's glory; or it has been regarded as a mere martyrdom of Christ consequent on something more precious, namely, His life and teaching; or even when it was made supreme it has been viewed as a mere exhibition or revelation. As revelation the cross has been viewed, on the one hand, as the crowning exhibition of Christ's personality, instead of the one effectual act and purpose of it. On the other hand, it has been viewed as the manifestation of God's justice, or of His love, or of the harmony of both. Instead of which it is the act of His holiness within both, and of holiness engaged in no mere revelation, but in the final judgment and destruction of sin in history. We can get little beyond an æsthetic, reflective, or sentimental religion from the cross if we treat it as a mere revelation instead of an act of redeeming judgment, loving and holy. We cannot get out of it a supreme social authority with power to bring its own kingdom to pass on earth. It cannot do for the course of history what it did at a point in history—overcome the world. And this is really what is the matter with us. It is roses, roses all the way, and no rue. The effective source of a religion for such a Society as we face to-day is no mere manifestation of love. Evil is much more than manifest; it is active and effective. To cope with it our faith needs God's judgment act of holiness for all time and conscience. We need the presence of the Holy One in His action, judging and executing the evil power for good, and establishing itself at the moral root of things beyond our chance or change. Once for all He condemned sin in flesh. He executed it in human nature by a moral act secret in Himself. There are various aspects of Christ's work in the New Testament and elsewhere—sacrifice, satisfaction, and its moving moral appeal to men's souls. But this aspect of redeeming judgment is the function of the cross which is decisive for the social effect of Christianity. It makes it the moral authority for organizing into the Kingdom of God a Society which is, beyond all previous, complex, confused, egoist, and anti-Christian.

The ethic of Christian love is not founded on the unity of Humanity in Christ, but upon the unity of grace in Christ. It rests not upon the Incarnation, but upon an Atoning Redemption; not upon love which draws to its affinity for completion, but upon love which is drawn to its enemy to rescue and bless. Christ is not the culmination of what is best in man, but God's victory over the worst. Christian ethic springs neither from Christ's injunction alone, nor from humanitarian impulse alone, but from the frame of mind in the Church produced by the cross. It is applied sanctification which reads the time. It is the public sagacity of faith. And faith is the Bible-trained experience by the Church of a common and completed redemption by a Holy God. The Church is a Holy Church; but it is not so because of its actual sanctity or fraternity; it is so because of its choice by a Holy God, and its redemption by a Holy Christ. The members of the New Testament Church consist of "*called* Saints," not actual. It is the calling that makes the sanctity and educates it. The bride grows to meet the husband who chose her and whose rank she takes. Whom God called He also sanctified, and He has gone on sanctifying. Indeed, it is actually a holier Church to-day than in the first century. And its Gospel is doing more to moralize society, and to rear a Christian wisdom for the age.

VII

I am afraid some will hear with impatience this suggestion of cause and effect. Theological theories have no such action on public practice, it will be said. No, they do not have it at once, but they do have it. They have a vast influence on the Church, and through the Church on Society. (I admit they are the convictions and property of the Church or Churches as a whole, and not of each particular member or minister.) These are not theories that I have set out. It is no mere matter of opinion when we realize, or do not, the supreme revelation of the cross as the redeeming holiness of God. On such a subject differences are not theories, but principles. The truth here is not an intellectual opinion, but a moral verdict. Upon it at last depends the certainty that God's holiness will be established to rule the relations of men. What was supreme in the work of Christ will in the end be supreme among the works of man. For each belongs to the one moral world (there are not two), and if the social foundation in Christ be destroyed, what can even the righteous do in a few generations?

If the publicist especially think it too remote for practical purposes to connect the work of Christ on the cross with the economic constitution of Society, I would ask him to bear these things in mind. First, that on the scale of history economics are in the long run what ethics make them; and ethics are what they are made by Christ's cross as the central act of moral history in man and God. And, second, that history has always been shaped by ideas or geniuses that were on the scale of all time, and were, therefore, by faithless sight held irrelevant to the practical politics of each several hour. Thirdly, it is worth recalling here that the modern Constitutional State is the result of the great moral movement of the Reformation with its moral centre in the cross.

While as a further point there is this: Christ, in His fate, was either a martyr or a Redeemer. If He was but the protagonist of martyrs, then conscience in its holiest possible form was swamped by the world; and, if so, how can mere lapse of time give it victory in inferior forms? There is thus no hope of the moral victory of Society. Morality appears but a by-product of forces to which it must always yield at a crisis. And how could the tragedy of the holiest of the race then reconcile any conscience to the mighty power in things? The cross of Christ was, before all else, an offering made by God to His own holiness; it was the finished and effectual restitution of His holiness upon the ruins of the evil power. It was not a penal satisfaction holy and atoning, but a holy substitutionary atonement with a penal element. It has other aspects implicit, I know. You may view it as but a sacrifice offered by Christ to God instead of by God in Christ; or as a sacrifice offered even by God, but only as propitiatory to men; or it was but a laying down of His life for the cause or the brethren. Under these aspects He might be our priest or our proto-martyr, but one thing He would not be. He would not be our social Saviour. He would not have established a Kingdom, but only taken a great step towards it. And He would not be our Reconciler. For, as I say, how can it reconcile my conscience to the mighty power acting in men and things to see it crushing in the cross the holiest of my race? But if that crisis was the Holiest Himself asserting Himself in Holiest Christ; if He was securing His holiness against man's sins, for His own sake and for man's for ever, at the utmost conceivable moral price; then we have a sure foundation for endless moral effort in a holiness which may be wounded but cannot be shaken, nay, which remains redemptive for ever. And we have a moral fulcrum whereon to raise to such a moral height the whole society of the race. Christ was Redeemer or lost. But if He was Redeemer, He was in His crisis destroying once for all the worst enemy and tyrant of Society, that is, evil, through the obedience and victory of holiness. Not only *a* victory, whose fruits later men might lose, but *the* victory. Evil could only be destroyed by something which did more than assert holiness in history to its wicked face—something which really *set up* holiness in history upon evil's destruction. And this absolute victory of the cross would be meaningless if it did not carry with it in its detailed action on history the gradual establishment of relations perfectly moral, loving, and holy in the constitution of Society itself. It is Society that the Church must capture, not for the Church, but for this holy Gospel and God. And, therefore, what has to be overcome in a conquest so great is not selfishness merely as an individual vice, but more than that—the supremacy of an egoistic social organization. We have to replace what we have now, an Egoism tempered with fraternity, by what is to be, a fraternity evolved through Egoism.

IX

There are finer and higher moral ideals abroad to-day which I will not insist owe their origin to Christianity. Concede that they are purely humanitarian. They extend their claim upon the whole social system, and especially the economic system, which has come into our hands. Are these claims to be barred out at the very threshold of society? No. Well, but if they are allowed in at all, how far may they come? If they are granted entry, are they likely to be content with anything less than the recasting of the whole *ménage*? The answer to these questions depends on their religious root. How far are these ideals the principles of ethical holy love? In a word, how far do they give effect to the Gospel? How far are they the form forced from the moral nature of the Gospel by the actual exigencies of the social hour? Because I do not see anything but the Gospel which even pretends to offer moral corrective and control on such a scale as the most progressive and worldly parts of the world require. Thinkers, critics, or poets may dream of another way. But no other way works; else Positivism, with its fine ethic, would not be the spent force it is. None of the ethical movements have power to bring themselves to pass. I am sure man will be submerged in material civilization if the best moral principles of Society remain but canons or ideals of ethics, if they have not behind them a religion more positive than Positivism to force them into public life. Prosperity and progress are very well, but after all, they belong to the pagan side of life. And that is the underside. The upper side to which all the prophets bear witness, is righteousness and peace. Righteousness and peace are worth more than prosperity and progress—where worth is really settled at last. It is not prosperity, nor is it progress, unless it make for righteousness, love, and peace. And where in religion have these things already been secured and made spiritual realities waiting to come in? Where but in the cross of Christ, with its establishment of God in evil man, its accomplished reconciliation of holiness and history? That human dignity also which the progress of civilization so crushes—where is it to find an eternal guarantee but in the honour paid in

Christ's cross to a Holy God by humbled man? If God's honour come short, man's cannot stand. Where are we to get that deepening, that exaltation, that propulsion for our moral ideas which make them wide, searching, and exacting enough to reach the heart of every human relation? Where but in the foregone re-creation of all moral relations in the atoning cross? There are circles, as I have said, where the cross is regarded as but exhibitory, where God's love is detached from holy judgment and atonement, and is only associated with merciful and exemplary sacrifice. In those circles religion shows no small tendency to lose its dignity, and to run to the futile and the frail. But that is the badge of a private Church, and not a public. And it carries with it the belittlement of human life. It causes the amiable trivializing of all Christian interests. It causes a loss of respect from the leaders of public life and action. It is unfortunate that the numerical growth of the Free Churches coincided with their decay of interest or certainty as to the nature of Christ's work. If we bring a Gospel whose first charge at its centre in Christ is not the honouring of God's holiness, then the moral demand must slowly slacken; whole tracts of life will be exempted from it; the soul's worth will decline with our conception of God's requirement and the soul's price; and men will be more easily treated as tools in a great concern, or as pawns in a great game. Material progress, in the wake of invention and discovery, will trample over human sympathy, and progress itself in the end will succumb to some form of disintegration and anarchy. We shall move forward, like the Staubbach waterfall, into dust. The God we need is not one who simply satisfies the necessity of human thought or heart, but chiefly the demands of His own holy nature. He honours His own holiness at the cost of His own sacrifice. Whatever it cost the Son it cost His Father more. He is one who intervenes as the world's Saviour, not in spite of His holiness, but just because of a holiness which makes Him the God for the most wide and exalted moral faith. Holiness, I venture to repeat, does not rest on love, like a complexion, but love on holiness. Love is but the outgoing of holiness, for the creation of holy souls. And it is this insatiable holiness that is the source of Redemption. We need, indeed, a living, loving Christ, but we need more—a Christ whose mission was action, whose purpose was a deed, whose deed was final, and whose range was the redemption of the conscience to the uttermost, its actual reconciliation to nothing less than the holiness of God. The reconciliation of the cross was not to God's love alone, where we looked for just anger, but to His holiness, where we had thought of mere justice. (It is hard to reconcile even the Churches to-day to the holiness of God.) And what was in view was the reconciliation of mankind as a social fabric, a historic society. It was a reconciliation in history, both as to its source in the cross where the Kingdom came, and as to its goal in the Kingdom as it is yet to come. We need for the moral purposes of Society a Christ who redeems because He atones, and atones because He is holy, and is holy because He is God. Christ's redemption is as wide as His God-head. He secures social goodness because He incarnates and secures God's holiness. He satisfies and commands the evil conscience of mankind because of the satisfaction His holiness was to the holy conscience of God. The Holy God found Himself in the holiness of the cross, and in the same act established His Kingdom. How can we improve such a vast, wilful, dreadful world as this to any moral purpose except by the pattern shown on the Mount, except we believe that the final moral conquest is not in this world, but in a world unseen, where the righteousness we labour for is already holiness in being? And that absolute conquest took place really in the viewless victory by the death of Christ. It is to be consummated actually in the far-off Kingdom in the heavens. And the procession of its entry is the moralizing of intervening history. Life is explicable and manageable only by eternal life.

X

As a matter of fact, the historic effect of Christ's holy work was social at once. It was to create a Society. It crystallized in a Church. And the Church is the collective missionary of the world. Society can only be saved by a Society. Individual evangelism, detached and isolated, is half wasted. It is only by Christ's holy work, translated into the holy society of the Churches, that Society at large can be converted into the holy Kingdom of God. Society, of course, must grow ever more just and loving as it advances in moral civilization. But you cannot get that moral civilization, that justice or love, into Society without something more in God than love or justice, without holiness as the keynote of His action on the world. And when the central crucial act of history in Christ is taken home by the Christian public as an act essentially ethical and not legal, it is bound to produce the greatest ethical changes in a Society hitherto taught to view it as a forensic transaction, a pathetic appeal, or an individual rescue. If "the supreme product of the Reformation is the modern State," what will the social product be of the reformed Reformation in which we are now engaged?

There is but one ethic, as there is but one God, one Christ, one conscience, and one moral relation of God to man. But many people have two ethics—a public or professional and a private. And why? Because the Church has never grasped as it has of late years that the centre of her creed is a person and a transaction wholly moral. The popular conception of it, the conception of many of the creeds, and of the majority of people, is metaphysical, forensic, or even commercial. Its salvation is, for the man in the pew, to say nothing of the man in the street, chiefly eschatological. It is salvage, as I say. It is only partly ethical. It is legalist; and it keeps Society on the legal level, to have such a religious centre. The old non-ethical and "hard-shell" orthodoxy, where divine justice is satisfied by penalty instead of divine holiness by sanctity, has tended to concur with a low public ethic. But when the public has really become possessed by that idea of Christ's work which I have indicated as ethical and holy, when the reasonable theologians have secured for it that hold on the public which some lowering legalist notions have too long kept, it is impossible to estimate the moral revolution that must take place in the idea of Society and its Christian perfection. Justice may be satisfied with penalty: but the only satisfaction to holiness is holiness. That satisfaction was made in Holy Christ, and it issued in a Holy Church. And as His work makes holier the Church it created, it must produce a mighty change in the social ethic of the faithful and through them on the moral constitution of Society.

2. IN THE MATTER OF PRACTICE

In passing to the practical side let me gather up my lines. The victory of the cross was the victory of holiness, which in Christianity has but a moral meaning. It was not the victory of the soul as pious, but of the soul as conscience. It was gained over egoism and guilt, and not over mere indifference or lovelessness. We have not too much piety, but rather too little conscience; not too much religion, but too little righteousness. The cross was, moreover, the victory of perfect holiness for an end of universal holiness. It was to reduce egoism everywhere to its proper place. It destroyed the prince of egoism, and goes on to destroy his realm in history. And it was to bring about this righteousness on the scale of Society, and secure the growth of moral personality to spiritual stature. It was for the holiness of Society in the ethical sense of the word holiness. It contemplates a Society in which the righteous holy genius of the Gospel regulates all the energies and relations of life. And it contemplates a Church whose soul and goal this charge must be. It is a conflict which means the reduction in each age of something which idolizes the ego at the cost of the soul, and of God. Yesterday it meant a challenge to feudalism. To-day it means a challenge to capital. But it does not challenge it as capital, only as an idol—as Mammon (and Mars)—as that which hampers moral growth in some, and makes it impossible in others. For instance, take landed capital. The worst condemnation of the present system of land tenure is not economic. It is ethical. It lies in the state in which it has left the moral personality of the labourer on the one hand and the landowner on the other, as a class. It must be a very lopsided Gospel and a very partial cross which has nothing to say to the present state of war—whether you take commercial or military war—which marks the capitalist age. So much by way of *résumé* and of forecast. Let me be explicit.

I

The life of Society contains two main elements. They are the economic and the moral. And the task of a worthy Government is always to appreciate and adjust these.

We may write off as ethical vulgarism the frame of mind which resents moral intrusion into public affairs—the mental condition, for instance, which tells the best of the clergy to mind their own business when they press the moral aspects of economic questions. That is just what they are doing. It is their business to apply a holy faith to the public conduct. To sever the economic question from the moral is to ruin both in the long run. A man is one, and has but one conscience. And such treatment of it is Jesuitical. It sets up a double morality, and it has a double code of honour for public and for private life. The economic question is far from being a mere stomach question; like every other great public issue, it is finally a moral one.

If illustrations of this truth are wanted, observe the ruinous economic effect of the immoral contempt for labour in classical antiquity. It meant slavery and social perdition. Or note the mischievous public effect of the contempt for the world in the middle ages. Or the effect of missions on social reform in India. Again, mark the industrial changes that are impending at this hour. They are due in very great measure to something moral, to the new sense of human worth and claim. The standard of living has a growing effect on wages, and, indeed, on the general distribution of wealth; and it is in its nature a moral standard and not a gastric. It is fixed by the moral ideas of the wage-receiving class. To raise wages, raise the moral standard of the earners. From this point of view the Gospel is the greatest of influences for a high wage. The social question grows yearly more urgent; but what is the social question? Is it not just the acute collision between a new moral ideal of human worth and a certain stage in economic development which thinks itself final? Again, note that labour itself, which produces wealth, whether in the labourer or his captain, is a moral quantity. Moreover, labour, on the great economic scale, is not possible without combination of some kind, which means relations between men, that is to say, moral relations. For such co-operation a moral culture is required capable of overcoming our natural egoism. The collective instinct is not natural for man as it is for ants and bees, which have no ego to assert itself in an anti-social way. Men are naturally gregarious, but they are not naturally collective. They draw together by a natural instinct, but it is no natural instinct that moves them to suppress their self-will for the common good.

Still further, the long course of economic history shows how largely the economic organization has been shaped by the prevailing moral ideas. With each increase of material and egoist power there came an extension of civilization, but only to be captured and mastered ere long by a higher moral and social ideal. In the lower stages men were mere machines, serfs, slaves. Labour was not a divine vocation for them. For slavery is not a calling. Even if they got a wage it was only for fuel to the engine. They were but "hands." But Christian ethic dignified labour. Monasticism gave it a new value, beyond fighting, for the whole of Europe. Calvinism taught its society that by God's choice the labourer's soul was as precious as a lord's, and more precious than a non-elect lord's. We have also the great contribution to industry of the puritan burgher. Then arose with Rousseau the philosophy of natural rights. There was such a thing as Humanity. And on this foundation there followed our present economy of liberty, fraternity, equality.

But what do we now find? We find this economy of individual liberty in due course reproducing the old materialism, the old egoism, on a larger scale. Careers were opened to talent. To him that had was given. Power rose to power. The weak went to the wall. The strong man was able to gather more than ever before. The equality of natural rights did not secure the rights of the weak and ungifted, who were yet souls and consciences after all. It was not an ethical or spiritual equality. It was not the moral equality of grace, but of Nature. It was only an equality of opportunities for men's varied natural gifts. That was the basis of the old Liberalism. Remove all obstacles to the capable man. Let the capable man become the man of capital. He used to be a war-lord, now he becomes a wealth-lord. The freedom of all for their natural rights ends only in the freedom of some. It gives scope only for the survival of the strongest, and the cult of the efficient "over-man."

The doctrine of the survival of the fittest is oligarchical; the fit are the few. The Free Trade doctrines which went through in the interest of the consumers (who include all) are now passing back into protection of the producers (who are but some), and this reversion is promoted chiefly by those producers who have thriven upon Free Trade. Is it not all a *reductio ad absurdum* of a freedom of natural rights? The rights-of-man movement ended in Napoleon. Republics, apart from sleepless moral vigilance, are in constant danger of a dictator. And a freedom merely natural tends always to the growth of monopoly, the aggrandizement of the already powerful, or, as it was called, the extension of empire.

Of course the industrial age has immensely increased human resource, dominion, and comfort. But it has huddled the masses, especially abroad, into a harder and bitterer poverty than before. (I am speaking in view of the world, and especially Europe, rather than of England). Accordingly it has called out the protest of Socialism, which demands, instead of an equality of opportunity, an equality of goods. An equal *opportunity* of enjoyment does not work, and so Socialism claims an equal *share* of enjoyment. Both Radicalism and Socialism stand on a morality; and they have on this basis deeply affected the economic system. But it is the morality of natural rights in both. They ignore that spiritual principle and destiny which is the only Christian basis of brotherhood. They are moral in a way—in so far as they give scope to an ego. But to an ego only as a natural force. They do not develop a moral ego, a character congruous with the redeemed and holy nature of Humanity. So there dawns upon the future the Christian moral idea of Society, and the duties of Society to the man without accumulative power, or without the productive power in present demand. There is a fresh protest against the tremendous tyranny of the immediate, the material, and the egotistic, which is the result of modern industry both in Capitalism and Socialism.

II

Can Christian ethic go beyond protest and cope with this dominion? Shall the Christian idea of social ethic affect economic conditions in the future as much as the morality of natural rights did in the French Revolution and the industrial? Well, it depends upon the Church, which has charge of that idea. Can the Church first make good a social moral principle out of her one message of redemption? I tried at the outset to show that it was inevitable that she should. And, then, can she carry it home to Society with all the force and authority of the Gospel? Can she make the moral power and dignity of her Gospel conquer the natural and egotist morals of Society? Can the Church so preach Christ's establishment of the public sanctity of God as to establish in public systems the sanctity of man as the redeemed of the Lord? Has she a cross to preach which can secure man's dignity by the first stress it lays on the holy honour of God and on the holy love which He has made the divine bond of Society? The question is not absurd. It is religion that shapes even economics at last. "Two people," says Ribot, "who do not worship the same God, do not till the soil alike." It must be so. Religion gives the main object of life, that is to say, the thing which confers final value on all material goods. Have we, then, a religion, a gospel, that can sanctify all material relations by the supreme place it gives to the moral holiness of God? Is there any doubt that we have? The only doubt is as to our fidelity.

We need the statesmanship of men who are not only Christians, but have a grasp of Christianity instead of a mere sympathy with it. Any statesmanship which has a mere political inspiration, and not one moral and religious, is without a compass, and may land anywhere. Even an apostle of the people on the old individualist and radical lines of natural rights may become a castaway. If a popular minister of the Gospel may be lost thus, it is not impossible for a popular minister of State. Indeed, is it not true that there is a special moral danger in taking up the cause of the people without religion? There are careers that show it. There are noble men who with faith would have been the leaders that we need above all else. We have the man if he had but our God. And, on the other hand, there are what seem strange conversions, perversions, and reprobations. But they are not really conversions at all, but simply violent reversions to type. Or they are cases of arrested development while the moral idea moves on. They are more than a personal idiosyncrasy. They are there in thousands. They make up half a party in the State. They thus represent the working out to its consequences of a certain conception of politics, one non-moral from the first, and expedient only. And they stand out sharp in the dawn of our new moral ideals of public things. Is it so strange that a non-moral nature should gravitate to the cause or party which resents moral considerations as intruders in politics, and courts the power of non-moral capital? Is it so strange that minds only economic in their build and range, with nothing but a business training, no culture and no faith, should be swept away by such mighty economic forces as are now at play? Is it wonderful that such minds should dream of an empire of vastness rather than worth, for want of an ethic anchored in the eternal principles of a religion moral unto holiness? Many of us would be victims of empire had we not been devotees of the Kingdom.

In such a spectacle we can look away from personal considerations and see the suicide of the old Liberalism, and even of the old Radicalism, which was based on individual rights and issued in unqualified competition. It is becoming an anachronism beside the new social mind with which the Churches and their Gospel have so much to do. The long eclipse of Liberalism means more than a party's exclusion from power. It means the beginning of the end of an age. It means a new Liberalism. The motto of the industrial stage of development was *laissez faire*. It was that principle in the old Liberalism which organized the victory of Capitalism. But the results of this victory have turned and rent that party form. Liberalism by its freedom of economic concentration made the plutocracy, which then left it, and left it without funds, and without a very clear programme so far. But in others this Liberalism has provoked a reaction against its *morale*. There are many who cannot believe that a moral society could be a mere mosaic of free egoisms tempered by charity or patriotism. They say, with Christianity, that society then becomes a field of hostilities, desolated by a war of classes, and even of nations. The sight of huge capital alongside of huge misery, of over-production on the one side and starvation on the other, has its slow moral effect on the public. And many, like Bishop Gore, are driven into sympathy with Labour, not so much, perhaps, from faith in the labourers as from a desire to raise a protest and a power to balance the social perils of immense private wealth in non-moral hands.

The temper of the hour is Collectivist. We see it in Trusts on the one hand, in Trades Unions on the other. Further developments of the kind must come, and doubtless errors; for we are not yet morally ready for a power so new as Collectivism. But the economic system has entered the moral zone. The economic view of history is always one-sided till it recognize the moral, and recognize it as the upper side. But human action becomes moral and permanent when we consider the future, and sacrifice to it with faith's courage and holy love. And it becomes the more moral the greater our future is. But the Christian future is great Eternity. It is not Time that carries Eternity, but Eternity that carries Time. The Eternal is the root of the ethical. And our Eternal is the holy person of our present

Christ, who is the image and action of Holy God. It is a Christian and holy ethic that has the reversion of the long economic future. The nineteenth century changed the world more than any other. What is to change the twentieth century? Why, that which will rule the final century—something that speaks out of the first.

III

Christianity has in the main taken an attitude on this question. The Bible, both in the Old and New Testaments, shows an anti-capitalist tendency. The prophets stood for the poor (by which, of course, were not meant the destitute, but the very small capitalists and labourers). Christ is more impressed with the moral dangers of wealth than with the Christian possibilities it has shown in the hands of many fine Christians of recent times. The early Church did not treat property with modern respect. And as the Church grew rich the protest broke out in Monasticism. The monks gave Christian dignity to work instead of war. "They taught Europe to work." They gave labour a divine position. They began what took effect far later in the abolition of slavery. They prospered. And what could they do with their wealth but hoard it? Money did not then make money. Interest, unfortunately, was all but forbidden. And so as Monasticism grew rich the Christian protest broke out anew in the Reformation. Luther extended the moralization of labour far beyond the limits of the monastic life. He railed and stormed, as his way was, against capital. The burgher and the farmer were his ideals. He dreaded the effect of the mass of wealth pouring into Europe from the discovery of the Indies and America. He took a violent stand against the powerful bankers of the day, like the Fuggers. Interest, he said, was mere usury. But the new development was too great for any number of Luthers to arrest. Then came the eighteenth century with its doctrine of natural rights and individual freedom, especially for the capable. Capitalism, as I have shown, took a new and mighty development on this base. But do you wonder at the current misgiving about it in a Christianity that must always be more engaged with natural wickedness than with natural righteousness?

The high finance which Luther dreaded has come to be the ruling power of the present stage of history. Capital is cosmopolitan. A nation may gain brilliant victories by land or sea, but it will be worn down at last by the nation that has the staying power of the purse. It is the leaders of finance that have the decisive influence in the actual politics of the West. Capital is the true International, and gold the true Yellow Peril. What is the relation between this world-power of Capital and the holy ethic of a world-gospel like Christianity?

IV

Let it first be clear what the question is. It is not one of individual ethics. It is not as if we asked, "Can a Christian be a Capitalist?" Of course he can. Many great capitalists are Christians, and great Christians too. Nor is it, "How shall a Capitalist behave?" That depends on circumstances as well as principles; and we had better be chary either of dogmatizing or denouncing. The question is about a certain economical stage or institution in the light of a final moral power. It refers not to capitalists, but to Capitalism, to Capital as the ruling factor in civilization, and in modern civilization especially. By Capitalism is chiefly meant the possession of the means of production on a concentrated and colossal scale by private hands, instead of by the whole body of the workers—including naturally those who work as financial geniuses, or as directors of work. And it is asked, how does the present place of Capitalism comport with the Christian social idea? I do not ask how it fits the precepts of Christianity, but how it fits the social principles of the Gospel in the interest of moral personality and of the moral relations between class and class, man and man. My contrast is not between Christ and Capitalists, but between Christianity and Capitalism.

Again, I cannot make it too clear that the antithesis I have in view is not exactly one between Capital and Labour. That is a false division. The great capitalists are among the greatest of toilers, whether in amount or in kind. And many labourers are capitalists. Nor is the collision one between private capital and social in the way of sweeping reconstruction. That issue is not practical. What is practical is the issue between the material and the moral element in our economic civilization, between Egoism and Christianity, between Capitalism and Society, Capitalism and Manhood or Soul, whether in the financier or the artisan. Man is more than his work, his commerce, his greatest achievements or civilizations, however great. Capital may remain private under regulations securing the best public good for the hour. By Capitalism, therefore, is not meant private possession alone, but what you have in Trusts for instance, the autonomy of Capital, the supremacy of capital intensely concentrated on a moral basis of egoism, a basis which is pagan as distinguished from Christian and fraternal. By this egoism, again, is not meant selfishness, but the individualism which has been the basis of industrial energy so far, and of the competitive system. On such a basis war is but the military outcrop of the principles that underlie our industrial peace. The inquiry, therefore, concerns nothing personal, only the features of a system. And the question raised is whether in economics production can be carried on in a constitutional way, by due representation in its control of all the interests directly concerned, or only in the patriarchal way which has been outgrown in politics. It is not a question as to the abolition of Capitalism, but its disestablishment. We know what a blessing that would be to the Church of Christ. Would it be a curse to the Church of Mammon?

Then, let it be clear further that Capitalism is a stage beneficial and essential in the providential conduct of the world. It is a real advance upon the powers that held sway before. It has made all civilized nations more productive than they could have been otherwise. It has developed resources in man and nature which all previous forms of Society had ignored or repressed. It has made man more of a moral being by laying stress on action rather than on enjoyment, on production than on consumption. It has done great things in the development of human freedom, human personality, and human happiness. It has given scope for free competition and worthy rivalry. It has set up a world-trade instead of a local, and developed that facility of human intercourse so necessary for brotherhood. After all, civilization has more promise than nomadism, and industry than agriculture. The present capitalist system, with all its defects, is, as a historic stage, better than the feudal, or the stage of domestic industries and hand-power. And it gives us courage to hope for a better stage still by its means. The very spread of missions has been made possible by it. It is impossible, if we watch God's way with the race, or with a man, to deny a true evolutionary place to egoism. And so with Capitalism, which is based on egoism, and which is meant to be but a stage in the Kingdom of God. It has been remarked that without Capitalism, Socialism itself could not have existed. The capital, the human and material resource, would not have been there to reorganize.

Up to a point Capitalism has done all that, and more like it that could be detailed. But it has also gone beyond that point. It has begun in its own interests seriously to limit freedom. Brotherhood promotes brotherhood, but competition destroys competition. Its energy is turning into the passion for power. Trusts and syndicates are extinguishing free competition, and turning employers into managers. We are threatened with a society of officials instead of venturers. Freedom of contract between buyer and seller is becoming a mere name in the case of the greatest industries. The smaller concerns are deliberately frozen out by selling below cost. And the like freedom is vanishing where the commodity is labour—between employer and employed. A monopolist trust can force the workman to choose between its terms and starvation. And so with the shopkeeper. The shops become tied houses. The small trader is becoming one of the most harassed and pitiable figures in civilization; and I confess I often feel more compassion for the little shopkeeper than for the unemployed to whom he is often so good. Commerce upon such huge lines is becoming a vast non-moral machine, whose tendency, taken by itself, is immoral. I mean by that, first, that its tendency is against the production of character and initiative; a drift which can only be arrested by the infusion of a greater volume than ever of moral force from some outside source. But, second, is not this true, that business honour hardly tends to grow by the change of local trade into world trade? And in the hands of corporations without a common conscience the possession of vast financial power may be more demoralizing than competition itself was.

V

It all pushes home the question. Where is the mighty source of supply for the moral control which is ever more needed as the scale of operations enlarges? The Christian Church is the great factory (if the word may be pardoned) for the men required. But is the Church supplying what is required in the measure required? We need guiding principles for the large scale of business and for high finance. And we need a skilled and duly-informed application of them. Is the Church supplying that special guidance? What is it doing to help men to adjust gold and the Gospel, faith and finance, love and egoism? It is a very difficult matter. It is not enough to say that the love and faith of Christ will keep a man right. They will not give individual men moral insight on the scale of a whole civilization. They will enable a man to make the Christian best of the current system individually. A billionaire at the head of a vast monopoly may be a sincere Christian, nay, a generous and lavish Christian. But his simple personal faith will not of itself give him the power and insight to apply the Christian moral principle to the accepted standard of the age. And as a matter of fact such faith has had more effect on the disposal of wealth than on the moral making of it. The current ethic of giving may be far more Christian than that of getting. Some of the truest believers and lovers of Christ are harassed by the way they are involved in an egoist system of accumulation. And how many more are entirely mammonized by it? The pursuit of wealth as the one object in life can be more fatal to the soul than bouts of vice. Every age has shown that, and the New Testament age among the rest, as we see in the warnings of New Testament teaching. But here is the difficulty. What we have to face is something which did not exist in New Testament times or lands, and is not dealt with in its precepts. It is the immense productive concentration of wealth, its accumulation for the purpose of fresh production, not for mere consumption nor for hoarding. It is the function of wealth making wealth. That is what is not contemplated even in the teaching of Jesus. In so far as He contemplates accumulated capital it is hoarded capital, for consumption only. And He dreads it. What would His judgment have been in view of the modern productive use of wealth? Would He have extended His proscription of laying up earthly treasure to modern banking? Or His depreciation of concern for the morrow to modern speculation? This is where godly and prosperous men feel a difficulty that needs at least discussion. And it is in such matters that popular Christianity, even in earnest men, fails to meet the real spiritual needs of the age.

Would it not be true to say that the conflict is coming to be not so much between Capital and Labour as between the great capitalist in every line of life and the small, between Capital and Society, Capitalism and the Public? The great financiers are coming to control not only the money, but the necessaries of life (corn, cotton, oil, iron, and the like), of the production of which they understand nothing whatever. This is especially possible in protectionist countries. So strong is their position as against the public that an alarmist article in a great paper (however it might be inspired) as to sudden critical relations with a foreign power may enable a large financial house to clear enormous sums in a day. This is surely an anti-social state of things. It raises the question whether such power can safely be left by any society that cares for souls in the hands of private egoism. Many such men, of course, are above abusing it. Many of these houses have a fine sense of honour. I know of one such in London, which financed, to the extent of a million, an American railway which soon defaulted. The house paid its clients the interest out of its own pocket till the concern was pulled round. And many use their great and lawful wealth nobly in the way of giving. The house I mean does, as you would know at once if I only named it. But many do abuse their power, and there is no guarantee that any number may not. Society may be pardoned, therefore, if it ask for protection by some moral authority; or if it dream of a more moral situation by ethical change in the economic system. It must be left to statesmen to devise the means; but a body so concerned with the moral well-being of society as the Church should not be idle in the matter, nor be briefed for the traditional side alone.

VI

I wish to repeat my sense of the extreme difficulty of the problem. A long series of indictments has been drawn out against Capitalism as non-ethical and anti-social. A dismal catalogue has been compiled of its social by-products in the shape of human poverty, misery, and bitterness. And it is all true. But another list is compiled (as we have seen) of the benefits it has brought to society in the development of human comfort, resource, and intimacy. And that is just as true. It has caused great irreligion. True. It has rendered great service to religion. No less true. What is the explanation? Clearly, it is a historic explanation. We have passed the summit of one historic ascent. We are beginning the down grade towards the next. The system is beneficial compared with what preceded, but it is on the point of being outgrown by another whose light reveals its defects. The existing order is developing the long-latent conditions of its own dissolution. It came with the sentence of death in itself, in its egoism. It was wound up to go but for a time and to serve a purpose. It has done a great life-work, but it begins to be demoralized with its own success, and it is bringing about its own end. It has no divine charter of perpetuity any more than feudalism had. Social needs are emerging which it cannot meet; social ills which its boons can no longer cure; moral claims which it can no longer satisfy; and moral ideals which make it look small. All these things, the new needs, sensibilities, and moral ideals, are being daily created by the Christian Gospel of man's value—his infinite, moral, holy value against worlds, and his divine moral redemption. The

Christian principle and ideal are gathering social force. The Church spreads the power of such a revolutionary Gospel by every soul it saves. Is it not time that it gave more thought to the guidance of that power? The same Gospel which provides the power must provide also the moral direction of it, else it must make way for another Gospel that will do both. A Gospel of the holy love of God and man surely contains the moral principle of social conduct no less than of a catholic faith. But the Church has been somewhat backward in developing those social principles, for reasons I cannot stay to specify. And so it has lost moral authority, especially for those active minds that not only act, but crave to act on principles, if they can be provided.

If the Church do not save the situation, directly or indirectly, it cannot be saved. But it must be done by the moral influence of the Church's Gospel, not by the prestige of the Church as an institution. The Gospel is the only moral force which has power upon a scale to subdue inordinate egoism. If Christ had His own in every soul, the capital of rich and poor would be His servant for the public good. It would mean great measures. Great measures flow from great men, or from great faith on the part of masses of men. And great men must be great consciences in the coming time. And their holiness is not only intense and simple piety, but insight into the deep moral condition of our collective life. But this means that the Church must give more of her best attention to these questions, both in their business and their moral aspects. We blame men for living with one conscience in two compartments. But is the Church single-eyed? Is her faith and thought making it possible for men to live differently? Is she taking pains to work out a solution of their difficulty, and guide them the moral way out? She claims moral authority. But her authority must be according to knowledge, and her advocates properly instructed. We have enough of ideal ethic, and of the cheap ethic of indignation.

We want an ethic of information, both as to the cross and the world. We must know fully our own Gospel, the historic situation, and business facts and methods. We must put our case in a way to appeal to the best minds and consciences of commerce. The current, forcible-feeble type of Christianity must take a form more likely to appeal to the strong and right-minded men among the leaders of the active world. It is these that we of the Free Churches are in some danger of alienating by a certain stridency of wrath, an impatience, an ignorance of the conditions of the case, and, above all, an inability to show the way out. Our most prominent voices do not always measure the whole situation. Some are quite intelligent but do not think, or they read and do not study. We must take pains to add to our evangelical fervour and pity an insight into the social implications of the Gospel on the one hand, and into the actual process of affairs on the other. At any rate the Church at large must do this. It must provide at least *some* authoritative voices who can speak on its behalf out of the fullness of their holy faith, to the strength, and not to the weakness, of the busy world. They should be Christian experts on the moral problems created by the economic life.

VII

Let me take an instance of what I mean. The Church has not kept its teaching up to date on one moral and social subject—the service of God in our calling in life, or what is theologically known as the doctrine of vocation. The views of stray preachers do not count for enough. It needs a Church doctrine. And that doctrine has never been seriously revised since the Reformation. The Reformation teaching on the subject was the great new contribution of Luther to the social ethic of his time. "You can and must," he said, "serve God in your daily calling as surely and truly as in your religious acts, or in a whole life devoted to religious pursuits and company." Now in the face of Monasticism that was a great and bold moral development. The monk was no nearer God than the godly house-father, burgher, or farmer. The sanctity of daily duty and calling was the great Reformation principle for Christian practice. We keep repeating it to this day. Our liberal and practical young preachers have urged it earnestly. But somehow it has been with disappointing effect. There is something that makes it unconvincing, something that makes it too much of a pulpit theme. How is this?

The fact is we have come to think differently from the Reformers on such things. We inhabit a totally different economic world. Their situation is not ours. Then everybody belonged to some Church; now multitudes in all ranks care for none. Again, we have passed from closed areas of trade to an illimitable world-trade. We have passed from Luther's world of consumption to a world of production. What we make becomes a huge engine for producing more in a rapidly ascending ratio. This surely calls for a new departure in the way of moral definition and Christian duty.

And then what confronts us is not Monasticism. It is not the monk, but the financier. It is not religious sloth, but colossal and sleepless energy in a tensely-knit world. Put yourself in the place of a business man who from his Sunday must plunge into the tremendous bustle and battle of competition in the great centres of commercial life. His work is not to serve humanity, but to make money, or to snatch a living out of a crowd of those who do nothing else. He must adjust himself to them if he seeks only to provide for age, illness, or family—far more if he seek a large fortune. He is a wheel in a system which has this for its principle. May he, then, feel that he is serving God as truly in these hours as in the hour of worship when he is stirred by the great vision of the city of God? Is money-making in itself a Divine vocation? Is it legalized at Christian law by its being for wife and children? Do not even the heathen so? I am not asking in scorn. I am stating a difficulty which exercises many of the good and able men involved, and on which it is easy for the ignorant and blatant to take lofty rhetorical ground. It is a question to which the Church as the custodian of Christian ethics is not yet prepared with a plain answer. Take, again, a prominent politician or statesman, who must have office if he is to do anything practical for ideal principles. It is a vocation for which he has divine gifts. May he feel he is serving God by the steps that are too often forced upon him if he is to win and keep popular power, the compromises he must make or wink at, the wrongs he must see in his party as if he saw them not? Take the vocation of the ecclesiastical politician—the bishop. Take the last Education Act.[1] It was admitted by a high-minded bishop who had much to do with its origin that it was an injustice to his opponents, but he said that it was the only way to cure what he considered a greater injustice to his Church. Does Christian morality permit that way of curing the injustice we suffer by injustice we do? Luther said in a wild moment that it looked as if God sent rogues to punish rogues. May the bishop feel that in thus securing the only true Church, where he has his vocation, he is serving God, as really as in the acts of piety and benevolence of which he is a most deserving pillar? Or has his Church deflected his conscience, as ascendancy always does? Or take the preacher who feels he can get so much wider a platform for his admirable Gospel by acting and talking to the gallery, and tuning his mode to the level of the crowd or the Press. How far may he go on God's service in the way of compromise between the spiritual vocation and the popular ear? Again I do not speak in scorn; but I voice a real perplexity. Or take this case, as I have named the Press. What has the Christian ethic of the Church to say in the way of

[1] 1902.

helping an editor who is forced to put his circulation before his education of the public, to give them what they like and not what they need; or a writer on the staff who must either lose his position in a crowded profession or write to the order of an unprincipled capitalist who has bought his paper? May he serve God in his vocation by selling his skill to present the best case for either side, as a barrister may honourably do? It opens the whole question, so large and so new, of the position of the Press as public guide under the ascendency of capitalists without conviction. Is the Press a mere newsmonger or a public guide, a caterer or a preacher, an industry or a profession? And if it is the former only, ought it to look for the respect which belongs only to the latter? Take another case, and a very different one. Take a poor cabman who has to be out at night driving fares to houses and for objects he knows to be wicked. Take a poor waiter who has to serve such people at midnight supper-houses, and who may thus be an unwilling, though not an unwitting, accomplice. There is no dishonesty involved. They are not asked to tell lies in order to sell things. Each pursues his calling. May he feel he serves God in it? Take a public executioner. Or take the detective who follows a profession which is useful to society as we find it by means which often borrow from the wiles of his quarry. May he invoke God's blessing on his calling and the ruses of war it involves? I do not here raise the whole case of war and its partial arrest of moral obligations. It is too large a question. But take the honest innkeeper, who is identified willy-nilly with that drink interest which is on the whole only one grade above the criminals it does most to make. Take the copying-clerk, who is not asked to do anything dishonest, but knows he is in the service of a concern that could not live by quite honest means. Or a Birmingham artisan who makes idols for India. Or a teetotal engineer whose firm is offered the contract for the machinery of a distillery. May these feel they are serving God in their calling? And how many such cases there are.

You say, let them leave their business. Let them go out like Abraham in faith, not knowing where. But, in the first place, the first moral charge on the Church is not these individuals, but the social situation which creates their difficulty. And in the next it is easy to say, leave the place. It might be easy to do it if you would provide them with a new livelihood. One day the Church may be able to do that, and back its strict standard by effectual help. But as yet it cannot. These men have wives and children, and duties to them. When Abraham went out, not knowing whither, he was able to take his establishment with him. It was emigration, not eviction. He was comparatively a free man as a man of means, which he took with him. His pang was not leaving a living, but leaving his native land and the land of his local ancestral God. But these people are not free. They are, like the vast mass of employees outside the organized trades, in economic dependence. Whereas the traditional Protestant ethic is an ethic of the independent, of the burgher and small master in a more sparse and leisurely age. There was not the social gulf then between master and servant. And there was no overcrowding. There were not then 300 men answering one advertisement. Luther's public were more or less substantial people. It was not a case of complying or starving. The journeyman's services could easily be transferred if the conditions were irksome. The master's terror of losing custom was not then what it is now. It was a time when there was a practical congruity between the moral idea and the conditions of men's calling. They could be good through their calling, and not in spite of it.

Besides, look at this aspect of the matter. Owing to the urgent conditions of modern life a calling has now to be chosen very early, and before aptitudes are revealed; and that means there is less chance of finding ourselves in a vocation which we can be sure is God's will for us, and in which we can serve Him with our whole heart, as we do in prayer, praise, or brotherly help.

Furthermore, there was not then the modern division of labour. A man could put his whole moral self into the article he began and finished. Work had character, and developed character, in a way that is impossible now, when the work is drudgery, and the workman is a machine which turns out but a fragment of the article, and is, therefore, not responsible for its success. We can, of course, serve God by drudgery. We have all to include some of it in our service. But can we do so with any moral result by a lifetime of drudgery which we keenly feel to be such, or only lose that feeling by becoming dumpish? Can a lifelong drudge serve God in his work as truly as in worship? Is his work his vocation? Can he put any hope into it? Must he not seek outside of it the zest that makes life worth living—and mostly in the excitement of sport, gambling, intrigue, or alcohol?

Christian ethics cannot be satisfied with calling on such people to glorify God in their station. It must go on to promote such a reorganization of industry as may give the worker freedom to live and hope as a man should, to keep a secure home and property, and become, in some sense, a responsible partner in the industry of which he is so great a part. This cannot be done simply by the goodwill of certain employers; it involves a gradual change of the whole system, under the ethical influences which it is the business of a Church that understands its business, its Gospel, and its world, to foster. It carries with it, of course, a new personal relation between employer and employed, and a change on both sides. Exaction must cease on the one side, and "ca' canny" on the other. There must be a mutual respect for personal dignity and a common respect for social duty. Both the soul and the brotherhood must acquire a new weight and claim. Christian love must give up some cooing and go to business. It must take the industrial form, which is more principle than sentiment. And it must follow economic and not philanthropic methods alone. I have pointed out how impossible it is to seclude economics from such moral control.

VII

There is the more need that the Church should bestir itself because these problems (and others, like the question of the unemployed), I am afraid, are insoluble in the present organization of Society. To step out of an awkward situation involves about as many moral difficulties as to stay in. The individual, therefore, whether master or servant, is not to be denounced if he honestly think it wise in practice to compromise, to bow in the house of Mammon so far as is consistent with being a useful member of Society, and working for the better day. There is certainly too much inconsistency that should not be; but also there is much juvenile nonsense talked about inconsistency. The Church at least should turn more of its attention from individuals to the order of Society which creates the difficulty. It is a very large task. It calls for a largeness of outlook which is lost in what I may call the granular Church theory of the old Independency, with its cellular notion of Society. And it calls for solid conviction and courage. It is in the nature of a social revolution, based on a moral. It is not simply a case of bespeaking public sympathy for the hard predicament of many consciences. It is not simply stirring the pity of the public for certain victims while all the time the same economic system works on. Nor is it merely pressing on Society the discouragement of certain practices, like commissions and bribes, or stimulating the zeal for righteousness, and the enthusiasm for certain public reforms that make for righteousness. That is very well and must not be neglected.

It is not simply helping the unemployed each winter, or covering the country with a network of wise organization for that excellent purpose. The unemployed are a symptom of social disease; and while we deal with the outbreak we must give more attention to the permanent cause. It is deep in our system. It is the whole social system that is involved in the crisis. And it is the passage to another social system that is the immediate problem. We are in the porch of that new system, or at least in the avenue. On every side there is a call for some real modification of unlimited Capitalism. In our own country the death duties and various schemes for a graduated income-tax point in the same way. The land question is only slumbering and gathering strength. And mindless wealth is producing Socialist sympathies where there is no belief in Socialist schemes. But these are only harbingers of something much more searching and radical, to which the ethic of a Christian brotherhood moves. There is no need for alarm. The change must come by the ethical conversion of society, and by no catastrophe. We must move by economic methods and on constitutional lines, with a moral base. And the Church must do more to inspire and guide that movement than she has done. She must herself change under her Gospel. No existing Church order is final any more than the social order. In the Church itself situations arise that strain the Christian conscience both in the matter of belief and practice. If extremists at one end ask whether a millionaire can be a Christian, extremists at the other ask if a minister can be a Christian. No form of Church life does full justice to the spiritual man. But the days of sect-making are over, like those of the cave-dwellers. We accept the best Church that our historic position offers, and we make the most of it towards the better time. So with society at large. For posterity's sake we cannot take a leap from the present into space. Martyrdom has often been debased to suicide. We may not at an impulse leave work, wife, and child and go out into the desert. There is always room for heroism and need for martyrs; but Puritanism may suffer from purists. Moral purity is not a white soul *in vacuo*. It means doing our best spiritual duty by the situation in which we are placed, and making it easier for those who come after us to do better. And it ought to resent martyrdom dictated and organized from without.

So the demand for a revision of the ethical doctrine of vocation is really one for the revision of existing Society and its organization. If the Church do not move in this direction all her blessed evangelism and priceless philanthropy will only leave her behind her Gospel, a private and not a public interest. She must revise the sources of her ethics, re-read the cross in its own growing light, reinterrogate the genius of the Gospel, and *by it* reconstruct historically the teaching of Christ. But it also means more. It means that her ethic shall be an expression of her collective Christian character as produced by the Gospel. It means still farther that she shall discern the time, and face social facts with due knowledge. She must go into the economic situation fully, and know it as well as the old prophets knew theirs, and better than the apostles. She must examine with real insight a vast field of social conditions. She must put fresh brain and conscience, time and money, into the task. She must abandon denunciation till she is in a position to offer the perplexed conscience some positive and practical guidance. It is not fair to the world to denounce without helping, or to help ignorantly. It is not the preachers only who raise these moral questions, or feel these misgivings about the present state of things. They are even more acutely raised and felt by many of the men whose duty lies in business, and who have made an honest success of it. Ministers especially should not take too superior ground on the subject. They should remember that they are set apart by the consent of business people into a somewhat sheltered position. They may not compete for a fortune, but, on the other hand, they are released from some of the burdens of such competition by those who are in the thick of it. It is seemlier, therefore, not to gird at those in the storm, but rather to study the stress of the time for their help. To hear some talk you would think that making money was a crime, and the whole end of business making money. It is not so. Trade with its profits is absolutely needful for the employment and comfort of mankind, and for eliciting the resources of both man and Nature. It is a contribution, or we may make it so, to the spirit of that same love which sustains, saves, and develops mankind. You have but to note how the development of commerce averts the awful famines that used to devastate miles and millions. No doubt business does offer great facilities for egoism. (Does it offer more than a graceless ministry?) The Stock Exchange does for gambling; but it is also a great agent to promote that mobility of capital which means so much for commerce and its boons. Dynamite lends itself to appalling social crimes, but we are not called on to blow up its factories. Do no merchants feel a pride in their calling similar to our own? Our Christian work is social reconciliation rather than denunciation. We ministers especially are set free in the flesh that we may be bound in the spirit. We are bound to wrestle for the present mind of the Holy Spirit of our Redemption, and to acquire that deepest knowledge of the moral world which comes in no other way. It is by the anointing of the Holy that we know all things. And what does that mean? It means that thus alone we know things on the universal scale, in their historic and their eternal setting. It is thus that we take the deepest and broadest measure of human affairs, and apply to them in the most relevant way the standard of the Eternal. To know men is one thing, to know man is another; and it is on man, not men, that society turns. The men of holiness have often been, and oftener been called, ignorant of the world's ways. Ignorant of its conventions no doubt often, but not ignorant of its true structure, of its most imperturbable laws, of its first conditions, and of its final destiny. Moreover, many of them have been mighty men in the world's ways and wars, and have intervened to decisive Christian purpose in its affairs.

IX

Let us work ourselves deeper into our faith, and think out its principles. Or let us trust ourselves more to those who really do so. It is not easy work. It is easy to be plain and obvious, but not easy to be a light in a dark place. The professors of the obvious are many and wearful, but the seers of the moral order are few. It is easy to yield to the religious impressionist, and I do not deny he has some ground for his existence; but he has none for monopoly, none for monarchy in the Church. It is not easy to grasp principles and go with them, as with torches, through the moral mist that surrounds us. It is not easy to track their action in a luminous path across life's moor. But then it is not easy to do anything worth much. And the Church has no business to be so fond of easy effects, so dazzled by rapid ones, or so facile in sympathy. No doubt her first business is to evangelize the world, and her second is to consecrate those she has evangelized, and her third is to help and heal those ignorant and out of the way. But it is a fourth, if it be not part of the others, to become the moral guide of Society, and translate her holy Gospel into large social ethics closely relevant to the time. Christ is made unto us first justification, then sanctification, then the redemption at the social end of all. I am afraid there are causes which make this task quite hard enough to tax a great religion of self-sacrifice. It is easy to secure public interest in religion and public help for charity; but it is not easy to get the religious world to educate its agents, to fit them to face the real moral issues of the time, or to elicit the ulterior moral resources of its own creed, either in the way of demand or of power. No grace of piety will save a Church for society without the grace of moral judgment and public sagacity. But the pious function of the Church is very apt to impede the righteous. And too many treat as mere morality the efforts of sagacious Christians to cure the public of its chronic enlargement of the heart and atrophy of the conscience.

It seems to me that we are near the end of what is morally possible for our magnificent philanthropy to do at the present stage of society, and that, without any slackening of Christian kindness, the situation demands a more searching inquiry as to Christian justice. Philanthropy can but deal with symptoms and effects; and we ought to get at causes. Moreover, the Church is becoming demoralized by its one-sided absorption in philanthropy. I am not speaking of the frequent effect on its recipients. Nor do I wish to chill a single effort in that direction. Christian philanthropy is the finest thing in history except the whole history of the Church. I only contend that is not the sole interest of the Gospel. And I have been impressed at times with the unhappy moral effect produced on the Churches by the necessity of keeping the favour of those most able to give. I could point to a case of a poor Church which has to part with its young minister because it cannot afford to part with a man of means who is riding over it with an excellent lads' club.

It is high time altogether that we prepared to take a more informed constructive attitude to public affairs than we have been driven to do. Our political party[1] has been for nearly a quarter of a century in opposition. Now this covers the formative period in the life of many of our young members. They have been educated by the excitement of platforms or partisans. These have their due place, of course. But they

[1] The Liberal Party, 1905.

should not exclude an education by deliberations or by Christian publicists. Our unhappy circumstances have immersed us in an atmosphere largely of indignation and too little of judgment. I do not wonder at the indignation. I share it. But without the judgment it will wreck us. It is a misfortune for us that our great assemblies are but mass meetings, and our popular press too hectic and scrappy. Our younger men have in public affairs grown up in a critical atmosphere, untempered and unsobered by practical responsibility, and unskilled in managing great affairs. Now, of course, it is the business of a political Opposition to oppose and criticize. But, in the first place, a great party ought to do so on a basis of positive principle which is prepared to become constructive as soon as it can. It ought not simply to be "agin the Government." And in the next place, a Church can least of all afford to be merely critical on public affairs. It has a spring of positive principle welling up into a more positive life. But we are too little aware of the treasure we possess. Many in our Churches have been infected by the reaction which for the last generation has ruled the world. If not sceptical of our great principles, they are not sure of them. And they do not always see their larger scope. Our ministers themselves are too often asking for guidance to be guides. That is because we do not educate them properly. What is meant by these Revivals in so many directions? They are a reaction against reaction. I hope they will lead us to a more constructive statement of our public position and demands all round than we have mostly put forth. For, in the third place, a party of principle should take itself in hand and aim at a practicable policy on which it can be solid for the time. We might put protest and denunciation to rest for a while. When practical and friendly statesmen ask us what we want, we ought to be more solid and practicable than they complain we are. We shall get nothing if we are not. Let us give our mind to the situation, and not only to the crowd. Let us deal with the statesmen, and not the politicians. Who reads, and who cares, what is done in Parliament now? It is outside Parliament that the vital issue lies; and even there it is not on those platforms where men are not heard unless they make us cheer. We want conferences, discussion in private, the practicable temper. Let us mix our prophetic passion with lay judgment. Let us not only take penalties, let us take some pains. We cannot enter practical politics except as practical men. I have no wish to see the public turn from us as hopeless irreconcilables.

And there is another point. It is a word to the politicians of our own side. Liberalism must make up its mind to very great changes, in which it cannot stand without religion, and cannot work. To talk and act as some Liberal politicians and journals do about the Churches is just the Liberal form of the other side's stupidity. And it is moral stupidity. That other side is, at least, not stupid enough to make the same mistake. It does realize the ally it may have in religion. Its instinct is not wrong. But its judgment is. It selects the wrong religion—wrong, not for party purposes (not at all amiss for these), but for public. The only kind of religion which can work Liberalism to its true issues for Society is the Christianity of the Free Churches. It was not accidental that in the great days of Liberalism, Nonconformity was its backbone. A free Gospel and a free Church are essential to a free State. How many that we have lost from our political side have gone from us in a cynical disappointment with movements on which they had built such hopes in youth! It is only the resources of a free Gospel in one form or another that can save the situation—whether with the Church or without.

One thing more. If Liberalism cannot do without the Free Churches, neither can it do without Labour. Nor can these Churches and Labour do without each other. There must be a better understanding. But an understanding. It is no understanding, it is a mere selfish bargain, if the working men vote for Disestablishment on condition that the Free Churches vote for the labour programme. All that belongs to the region of political concordats and caucuses. It is no understanding if the Church simply gratify the working class by adopting their measures, or if the working class gratify the Free Churches by nationalizing the schools. We want more than that. We want both sides to realize how indispensable each is to the welfare of Society and to the Kingdom of God. If Labour is bent only on doing the utmost for itself, and using the Church for that purpose as the highest bidder, then no understanding is possible. For a true Church that is no holy ambition. It is not there for itself, but for its Gospel and Kingdom. And a real understanding is not possible between self-seeking and self-sacrifice. It can only exist between parties who care more for something beyond themselves than for any aggrandisement of their class or their sect. How shall we give the masses of the people the sense that they belong to society like the rest, and have an equal interest in its order and progress to moral and even holy ends? We have received them politically, but it is a failure. Why? Because we have not gone far enough. We have not received them industrially, and only very partially in religion. It is an ethical regeneration of the whole nation that is required from the Churches. And by God's grace they will bring it (with some recasting of their own creed). What can regenerate a nation in that way but the Christianity that converted the nations, nursed them into nationality, and holds the secret of their moral dignity and power, the secret of the public conscience and soul? Nowhere outside Christianity can moral regeneration be found either for Church or State. The millennium for the worker rests on the moral principle which is the holy soul of the Church and the power of the Gospel. The Church, of course, must be what its

Gospel makes it. And this same Gospel that makes the Church holy is the only principle that can make Society either safe, just, or glorious. Let us not be content with a ministry of kindness, but of equity also. It is not a matter of almsgiving, but of giving ourselves, of going to neighbours, making them brothers, and making their interests our own, whether we adopt their schemes or not. Do not worry about Church statistics. It is a matter where the Church can afford to be indifferent to its own aggrandizement if it can but get access and influence with its Gospel. The Church's numbers can only be increased by thinking little about numbers and much more than we do about the Gospel. We need a better Gospel far more than we need more gospelling. And Church attendance will come, if we wait better upon the ministry of a wise, holy, searching, humbling, and kindling Gospel.

Our true capital is our moral capital, and our true leaders are those with the genius of the strategy of God's Kingdom. Even in the passing world the true capital is not money, mines, or lands. It is neither flocks, herds, millions, nor banks. It is not even labour. It is brains. It is ideas. It is conscience. It is justice. It is love. "The sheep of My pasture are men," saith the Lord. The poor are there for another purpose than to be exploited. All the resources of Nature were no wealth without men, without mind. Wealth means value to moral beings. So in the Church: its true capital is neither its traditions nor its institutions, neither its tithes, nor even its creeds. It is its holy faith and love and the sagacity of both for the social soul.

Holy Father! So increase our faith that by Thy Holy Church we may come into Thy holier Kingdom through the grace of Christ, who is the Holiest of all. Amen.

The Grace of The Gospel as the Moral Authority in The Church

PREFACE

I SHOULD like to offer at the outset a few theses in answer to the question, What is the authority over the Bible? They may guide the reader in the first part of the book.

1. There is something authoritative for the Bible itself.

2. It is not something which comes up to it from without like the scientific methods of the Higher Criticism. To make that supreme would be rationalism.

3. It is something which is in the Bible itself, provided by it, and provided nowhere else. We must go back to the Bible with modern scholarship to find what the Bible goes back to.

4. It is not truths extracted from the Bible and guaranteed by prophecy and miracle. That is the antiquated supernaturalism with its doctrinaire orthodoxy.

5. In a word, that is over the Bible which is over the Church and the Creeds. It is the Gospel of Grace, which produced Bible, Creed, and Church alike. And by the Gospel is meant primarily God's act of pure Grace for men, and only secondarily the act of men witnessing it for God in a Bible or a Church.

6. The Gospel was an experienced fact, a free, living, *preached* Word long before it was a fixed and written Word—as was the case also with the prophets.

7. It is not enough to say the authority in the Bible is Christ unless you are clear whether you mean the character of Christ or His Gospel. All admit Christ's character to be a product of God's action; is the same true of Christ's Gospel?

8. To apply the Gospel of Grace as the standard of the

Bible is to go higher than the Higher Criticism. It is the highest. The Gospel is not merely the final test of the Bible, but its supreme source; and the Bible is its humble vassal to be treated in any way that best obeys and serves it. The security of the Gospel gives us our critical freedom.

9. The Bible is not merely a record of the revelation. It is part of it. It is more true that God's great Word contains the Bible than that the Bible contains the Word. The Word in Christ needed exposition by the Bible. The Gospels find their only central interpretation in the Epistles.

10. The Bible is not so much a document as a sacrament. It is not primarily a voucher for the historian but a preacher for the soul. The Christ of the Gospels even is not a biographical Christ, so much as a preached Christ. The Bible is not so much a record of Christ as a record and a part of the preaching about Christ, which was the work of the Spirit and the apostles. There is no real collision between the Christ of the Gospels and the Christ of the Epistles. The apostles, and especially Paul, moved by the heavenly Christ, form an essential part of Christ's revelation of God's grace.

11. It was a theological Gospel, though not authoritative as dogma but as living, personal revelation. The Christian experience must cast itself more or less in the forms of its historic origin, and not merely in those of human relations and affections. *E.g.*, Christian sonship is not natural, or even spiritual, but evangelical; it is the sonship of adoption. So conversely with the Fatherhood of God.

12. This subordination of the Bible to the Gospel was the relation felt by Jesus Himself. He used His Bible for its Gospel, not for its information—as a means of grace, and not as a manual of Hebrew history. That is, He read His Bible as a whole. He commits us not to the whole Bible but to the Bible as a whole. The Bible is not a compendium of facts,

historic or theological, but the channel of redeeming grace. Faith is something more than the historic sense dealing with documents. It is the moral and spiritual sense dealing with revelation as Redemption.

13. The appeal of the Bible is not to the faith of the individual but to that of the whole Church, which is the other great product of the Gospel. My dullness or disbelief does not affect the witness of the saints, classic or common, in every Church and age.

14. In the Church the Bible becomes more than a product of the Word. It is a producer of it in turn. It generates the faith that generated it. As the greatest of preachers it produces preachers. And it is at home only in a Church whose first duty to men is to preach.

15. The detachment of faith from the Bible and from its daily use marks both Romanism and the religiosity of the modern mind.

16. The disuse of the Bible by Christians is due to a vague sense of insecurity rising from critical work on it, and to the extravagant claims made for it which criticism prunes.

17. The Christian creed has really but one article, great with all the rest. It is the Gospel of God's redeeming Grace in Christ. The charter of the Church is not the Bible, but Redemption. Those words of Christ are prime revelation to us, and of first obligation, which carry home to us the redeeming grace incarnate in His person and mission.

18. The Higher Criticism has been a great blessing, but it has gone too far alone, *i.e.*, without final reference to the highest, the synthetic standard of the Bible—the Gospel of Grace. What we need, to give us the real historic contents of the Bible, is not a History of the Religion of Israel, but of Redemption—with all the light the Higher Criticism can shed on it, and much more that it cannot.

19. Christianity will not stand or fall by its attitude to its documents, but by its attitude to its Gospel and to the soul.

20. The Free Churches have yet to face the spiritual problem created for them by the collapse of an inerrant Bible and the failure of an authoritative Church. And the only key lies in the authority of that grace which called them into being as the true heirs of the Reformation, the trustees of the Evangelical tradition, and the chief witnesses of the Holy Spirit of our Redemption.

THE GRACE OF THE GOSPEL AS THE MORAL AUTHORITY IN THE CHURCH

I HAVE already spoken of the Church as the moral authority of Society. I now venture to ask what is the moral authority of the Church? In the Church, as in society, the authority is a moral one; but in the Church it is a moral authority raised to the level of a religion whose whole issue turns on a holy redemption from universal moral lapse. So the answer I have to expound is this. The authority in the Church is the moral holy power of redeeming grace—the gospel of moral redemption by a God who saves rather than guides, and forgives rather than rewards. Buddhism is also a religion of redemption, so is modern pessimism. But Christianity is the religion of *moral* redemption, as the only ethical basis of a world that is more wrecked by sin than sorrow. Displace the centrality of sin in the natural world, or holiness in the supernatural, and Christianity (as a brilliant Frenchman says) "is a kind of rebus, an incoherent drama where you see a lifeboat launched to save a painted ship upon a painted ocean."

I

The subjects I propose to myself, Authority and the Church, are world-subjects. They are at the heart of the age's problem, and have been for many ages. And they are most closely connected. Without an authority there can be no Church. Without an authority final for the soul there can be no triumphant Church. And without a Church, authority has no effect.

But as with the Church to-day, so with the state and the soul. Authority ecclesiastical, civil, and religious is severely shaken. The Church idea has in many quarters among ourselves sunk low, in some it has vanished. Its authority appears to large numbers of people a mischievous anachronism. At the same time the existence of a non-moral and plutocratic Government has tended to diminish respect for civil authority. The abuse of law and constitution has lowered respect for both, and by so much it has fanned that passion for an unchartered freedom which marks our turbulent race in general and its youthful end in particular. Parental authority has almost ceased to exist. And to these anarchic influences I add another which drives many of our political and ecclesiastical opponents to snatch at the coarser authorities—I mean the critical spirit and method, applied to those standards of religious authority which have ruled us (and even made us) in the past. The broad effect for ourselves is this. We make on the public the impression of having no authority, religious or ecclesiastical, and of preferring to have none. We thus lose many of the best minds and elements of the time who are yet not hostile to the Gospel. We lose women especially. And people betake themselves from us to a Church that has, or believes and claims that it has, a palpable authority—be it no more than the late-born episcopate. Some do this as a refuge from disorder, some as a refuge from scepticism. Episcopal rule appeals to some who once took sad part in our church meetings. The authority of the creeds appeals to others who have tasted the effect of criticism on the Bible. Social ambitions I admit have their wretched play; but it is not these that draw from us the people we should most wish to keep.

If we have ceased to provide society with an authority we have ceased to be a Church, however much of a missionary society we may be; and we shall not be that long. If we are not clear about the reality of our reigning truths all our

Christian activity is brief and hollow fuss. A Church is made from above, and its message is from above. It *descends* on man and on man's conscience. It is only too easy, I know, for one Church to debase this truth into the spirit of ascendancy, and irritate another into spiritual anarchy. But the very curse that ascendancy brings to a Church is a witness to the thing it perverts—*corruptio optimi pessima*. The spirit of ascendancy is really the indispensable note of authority. It is harsh instead of gracious, domineering instead of governing, intrusive instead of welcome. But authority it is, none the less, that makes a Church—moral holy authority. It is not sympathies, fraternities, affinities, aspirations, enterprises. It is not even a common faith and love—that is too subjective to be authoritative—it is a common Lord of the conscience, a common King of the soul. The Church is not a democracy. Its native spirit is not the spirit of a democracy. Its assemblies are not public meetings where each stands on his equal right. Yet that is what we have come to. And it explains a great deal I am sorry we have come to. Our ecclesiastical rights are not to be defined by our membership of a Church, but by our membership of Christ. The Church is a Theocracy. Its gatherings are meetings of those who own a common worship and obedience. One stands in the midst, before whom our conscience has neither rights nor merits. He is an absolute King, and not an elected president. He is a judge, and not an arbiter; our owner not our champion; our Saviour, not our hero. We should behave as in a court, not an assembly. We do not greet Him, we worship. We do not accept His rulings, we tremble at His word and we glory in His grace. Yet in many of our Churches, while we have a convenient order for the conduct of our affairs, we have no due sense of this majesty. We do not stand in the real presence. And we have little power to impress it on the public. We give people interests and sympathies, and we draw them into connexion. But do we give them what mankind needs far more deeply than sympathy or help—what will serve them when these are out of reach? Do we give them what Rome gives in her way—what overawes the soul—a real authority and guide for life? I do not say we do not have it. With many individuals we do. But with many more whom we truly touch we touch but a side of their life, not its core. And we do not have the power in a corporate way, in a way to weld our Church individualism by it, or to stamp it on the society we live in. The public recognizes our human kindness, our good works, our spiritual earnestness, our zeal (wise or unwise) for social righteousness and political freedom, our sympathy at times for certain kinds of culture, and with all kinds of disability or misfortune. But it does not recognize in us the deep religious note of authority, of control, which Englishmen especially love, and love more than sympathy. I admit the public owns that note in cases where the authority is unsound. Its insight for authority is not so keen as its instinct. But in our case it scarcely owns it at all. And what is freedom without it?

But you demur. You say, "We certainly do not care for ecclesiastical authority, and we do not claim it. But we have, even ecclesiastically, the office of the ministry. Theologically we have a certain body of belief, though informal and, in cases, vague. And, religiously, we have the Bible." And so you raise questions supplementary to those of Authority and of a Church. You raise the questions of a Bible, a Ministry, a Theology, a Creed, and the Authority behind and above them all.

But you cry out at an authority behind and above the Bible or theology. Can a Protestant recognize an authority in theology? If so, where is its freedom? But others care less for freedom than for truth, and ask, Have we no such authority in the Bible? Can there be for a Protestant an authority behind that?

II

I must here leave the question of theology alone, only stating that Protestant theology is founded upon authority as much as Catholic, though in a different way; and I go to the question of the Bible. While some demur to an authority for theology lest we succumb to the moles and the bats, others wonder that there should be any question about it. "Of course there is an *authority* for conscience, theology, and the Church. And it is in history. *It is the Bible.*" And they are uneasy when I venture to include the Bible with Church, Ministry, and Creeds, and say that there is an authority beyond and above them all. An authority above and beyond the Bible! They must protest.

But another section says, "Yes, there is *something above the Bible*, but it is *in the Bible*. We must not go behind the Bible to find what is above it."—(They forget that, as I shall show you, there was something that was making Christianity, and the New Testament too, before a word of the New Testament appeared. They go on to say)—"The authority of the Bible is within it. We find in the Bible various parts of unequal value, and we select certain parts to be the authority for other parts, to be canonical within the canon." Now in one sense this is a great and sound Reformation principle of interpretation. The canon of the Reformation scholars was to take the clear passages and use them to test the obscure. That was to be the principle to guide the Church. Cranks and doctrinaires might fix on unique and obscure passages which fascinated their angular or mystic minds. They might puncture these texts and then colour the whole of the Bible with a dilution of the theosophy which oozed from them. To this day ill-taught and self-taught people frame amateur fantastic theologies in that way. And the poor churches are bewildered by the gropings of unfortunate men who were told at college only that they must make their own theology. Do you wonder that the result of such teaching is collapse for church or college? But the sound principle of old was otherwise. And it remains sound to-day. We should use the clear to interpret the obscure. But that is not exactly what they mean who say that the Bible must be read by way of a selection of certain parts. They would proceed by the way of dissection. They would act critically rather than hermeneutically. They would cut out certain pieces as being Bible, and discard certain others as intrusions on the Bible; and the discarded portions would not be interpreted by the rest, but rather neglected, and practically ejected from the canon. Now I hope to point out that *so far* from the true Word being a part of the Bible, the Bible is a part of the true Word. It is not the Bible that contains God's Word so much as God's Word that contains and uses the Bible. The Word is not in the Bible as a treasure hid in a field so that you can dig out the jewel and leave the soil. It grows from it like a tree. It breathes from it like a sweet savour. It streams up from it like an exhalation. It rises like the soul going to glory from its sacred dust. The Word of God is not to be dissected from the Bible, but to be distilled.

III

And another group takes up the tale, "Yes, dissection is what the higher critics practise, and it often seems arbitrary, and they do not all agree. Their standard seems to vary. They have no common authority. But really we do not know much about it. We are preachers not scholars. And we sometimes regret the time we were obliged to bestow on scholarship in the course of our professional education. Now we take *another standard for the Bible* than the natural selection of the scholars. Our principle is one of supernatural selection. It is a principle of emphasis rather than of criticism. *It is*

Christ. We can all get at that principle from our English Bibles alone without so much trouble. We will make piety do the work of learning. Our sacred instinct can dispense with so much education. We will go by an elective affinity. And whatever in the Bible sounds like Christ we take, and what does not we need not concern ourselves much about." Now here again we have the debasement of a good Reformation principle. It was Luther's. Only Luther was a great Bible scholar, both with head and heart. He dealt very freely with the New Testament. He was the first of the higher critics. He ejected *James* from the canon, and certain other books, because they did not, as he said, "ply Christ"— *Christum treiben*. But this is not quite a satisfactory principle to-day. Luther was open to the retort that what these books did not ply was Paul's conception of Christ on which Luther lived. He rejected *James* on Paul's authority rather than Christ's. And the burning question to-day is just this: Is Paul's conception of Christ compatible with the Christ of the Gospels? For our test are we to take the Christ of the Gospels or the whole Bible Christ?

But farther, suppose we confine ourselves to the Christ of the Gospels, modern criticism is as severely at work on these documents themselves as upon the Books of Moses. It claims to settle what is historical and what is not in the narratives out of which we frame our idea of Christ. Well, what is to guide it in doing that? It cannot take the Christ of the Gospels, because the very thing that is in question is the narrative out of which the idea of this Gospel Christ is to be framed. We cannot get the Christ of the Gospels till we have settled how much of the Gospels is left to work with. What is the standard by which you select the parts that are to yield you Christ as a standard? What obliges us to start with the axiom that everything the Gospels report about Christ is correct, when we have ceased to hold the infallibility of all parts of the Bible? But if everything in the Bible is not equally true, how are we to select from the evangelists the parts that make the true Christ? The real answer I am giving to the question is that the selective principle is the gospel of grace in Christ crucified. Whatever carries that home, whatever is indispensable for that, is of prime value and obligation. It seems very liberal and plausible to say Christ is the standard of the Bible, but we are evidently not quite clear about the conditions of the problem. I am reminded of a speaker who once stirred the admiration of my boyhood for the generous compass of his mind because he said his principle was "Make Christ your centre, and strike your circumference as wide as you like." But is not that like a great deal that passes for breadth when it is but vagueness, and for inspiration when it is no more than inflation? It misleads the public, but not those who know.

IV

If ever you hear such language as that, or are tempted to use it, might I beg you here and always to ask yourselves where you are? What do you really mean by Christ, and what by the Bible? Do not escape in a high mist of devoutness. What is the relation of the Bible to Christ? What is its function? Is the Bible, is the New Testament simply a historical document whose sole function is to give us a trusty report about a certain personality of supreme personal dignity and public consequence? Many people would at once say, "Yes, that is just what the Bible is—a historical document. We have escaped from the notion of its verbal infallibility, and we are escaping from the theological monopoly of Christ and its version of Him. We are in an age when the new historic spirit has taken command. It has rescued the prophets from the theologian; it must now rescue Christ. It has rehabilitated the Old Testament for history; it must do the like with the

New Testament and especially the Gospels. It must deliver the Gospels from the Epistles, and do something to correct the hoary overestimate by the Church of St Paul. We must treat the books of the Bible as other historic documents are treated. Their sole function is to give us sifted data for the one valuable thing—the personality of Christ. The Gospels about Jesus Christ are like the documents that tell us of King Alfred, and they are there simply to be handled in the same way. Approach the Bible as you would any other book: that is the way to use it if you would make it the layman's book. That is the simple way."

It is certainly the way of the simple, as the Book of Proverbs uses the word. Do you not see what you have done? In the first place you have taken it for granted that documentary criticism of the Gospels must leave us with the personality of Christ—which it has not always done, at least to the extent of leaving the Christ you want. And in the next place you have made the historic sense, and not faith, the proper response to the New Testament. You have not given the Bible to the layman. You have done exactly the opposite—you have taken it from him. You have made a present of it to a small aristocracy of experts, to the learned in origins, the experts of historic research. Have you not? These documents, as mere documents, are very difficult—far more so, from their age and their Orientalism, than any that deal with Alfred or Luther. The proper historic treatment of them is not every man's affair. It is work only for men of a special training high and delicate. Given the Bible to the layman! What you have done by making the Bible chiefly a document is, first, to make laymen of almost all believers lay and clerical; and then to deprive every such layman of the right to an independent judgment on the truth of the Bible, or a personal sense of its authority. We should all have to take our opinions from a clergy of historical experts. These would really be our authority. And I confess that for the purposes of faith I prefer the old clergy to the new, the priest, the theologian, to the mere scientific historical expert.

V

I will go farther. I will say that, compared with the mere critic of documents, it is the theologian that represents the rights of the laity. He defends their only *locus standi*. He stakes Christianity on something that can be verified not indeed by human nature, or by natural religion, but by a universal experience of grace, where preacher and theologian are all laymen, yet all experts, alike. To every man this penny. He puts it all upon the experienced Gospel of Grace, Redemption, and Forgiveness, in an atoning Cross. May I go into this?

Why is it that the Reformation has been the herald, the advance-guard of Democracy? Because, through being above all a theological movement, it made the pew the final appeal. It was the theologians, the makers of the Reformation, that also made the supremacy of the laity its Church principle. How was this possible? Possible! It was necessary, because they maintained that God's great gift in the Bible was not a documented character, but a preached Gospel. They said the great appeal of the Bible was not to the historic sense of some, but to the moral sense of all. It was definitely to the sense of guilt and the need of a Saviour. It was not vaguely to the religious sense, any more than straitly to the historic. It came with a *moral* historic redemption. It came to the religious sense in a very positive way—not in the way of aspirations or sympathies, ethics or convictions, but in the way of an act of grace calling out faith, of forgiveness crowning repentance, the cross creating a kingdom, the Spirit creating a Church. The Bible made its appeal to the moral sense as theological, *i.e.*, to morality as holiness facing sin. It did not set reason in the presence of truth but conscience in the presence of holiness. Its theology was the theology of the conscience, not of the schools—theology which had its centre not in philosophic thought but in the experienced forgiveness by historic grace of moral lapse. Its problems were not academic but personal. It was the theology inseparable from a positive Christian revelation, as distinct from the liberalism of mere natural religion with a Christian spirit. It was not the actual facts that the Reformers laid such stress on; nor was it on speculative theories by which later ages strove to adjust and explain the facts in a scheme of thought. It was upon the practical burthen and religious efficacy of these facts as set out in the Bible, in the New Testament especially. It was upon the permanent centrality of God's grace towards the sinner in Christ. It was on the Gospel. For them the Bible was not a historical document but an inspired. It was not there to provide us with a biography of Christ, or even loose memorabilia. The memoranda had a purpose in them far greater than biography. No biography of Christ in the modern sense is possible. The documents were never compiled for that end. They are too meagre, too elusive. Not one of the evangelists directly reveals that sense of development in Christ's mind or character which is indispensable to biography as we understand it. If we set about tracing such development we have to pick it out with great pains and dubiety. When *Hebrews* speaks of Christ's perfecting by suffering, it means not the culture of His character but the culmination, in His ever adequate character, of His work as Saviour.

And the Gospels were not there even to guarantee for a posterity of historians certain facts of Christ's life. In regard, for instance, to a fact so great and sure as the Resurrection of Christ, the man who says that no fact in history is so well attested by documentary evidence has no idea of what strict historic evidence means. In the way of testimony we have evidence which the mere student of records would regard but as secondary. We have indeed the very high evidence of a historic effect on the despairing Church which is otherwise inexplicable. But we have not the first-hand testimony of any one who actually saw the authentic body of Christ emerge from the rocky cell. The matter of first-rate moment is that Christ has risen, and lives, and all for our salvation. The real evidence that Christ is risen is something I can verify, who am little skilled in handling documents and assessing evidence. It is that I have had dealings with Him. It is like the evidence for the whole Bible. It is layman's evidence, not scientific but moral. It is the witness of the evangelical conscience, and of Christian experience to a risen Redeemer. The essential thing is not historic belief in the Resurrection of Jesus (which devils might believe and tremble), but moral faith in a risen Saviour. The real witness to the Bible is the believer's witness to the Gospel of which Christ's resurrection is an essential part. It is for a layman's gospel that the theologian stands, not for the historic facts in their scientific selves. It is for something that appeals to the sinful soul in his salvation, and not to any experts of a pursuit.

VI

I repeat, the Christian theologian is the champion of the Christian laity, the pleader and justifier of the general Christian experience. If he is repudiated, it is by a laity victimized by something feebler than the Gospel, or by an age that demands a biographical Christ for its interest instead of an evangelical Christ for its salvation. Bear in mind that the Reformation was the re-birth for ever of the long-lost Evangelical principle which *is* Christianity. It rediscovered the Gospel. It restored the supreme authority of grace for both faith and creed. Its method is not something superannuated—something that was still the victim of the theological stage, and that must now be superseded by the positivism of history. It was a great integral crisis in the onward moral movement of the general soul, comparable only to the discovery of the inductive method in science, and as little to be left behind. It was essential, not simply for its own time but for the whole Christian creed and future. Its Confessions are not simply milestones on the Christian road, which are now but historic and external to the Church, and which the Church has passed, and may forget. They were living products of the continuous spirit of the Church's best and the mind's best; and they are fountains still. Their principle and method are organic to Christian history, and perennial. It was the theologians of the Reformation that discovered and declared that the source and standard of Christian theology is one with the fundamental principle of Christian experience; that the test of theology is its capacity for being preached to the believer's soul; that the science of grace must commend itself to living faith in grace; that the dogmatic norm is identical with the religious authority in the Gospel. They make theology really religious. To every preacher of the Gospel his theology must be a part of his religion. He must know where he is. So the theologian of grace is the real mediator between the historic Christ and the present day. The chief value of Christ for the present is not as a historic figure of the first century reported in the Gospels. But He is above all things for us a Christ who by His work of grace now lives, saves, inspires, and rules in heaven and on earth. The Christ of the Gospels is not Christ the character but Christ the Saviour. If there is any selection among His words or deeds we must select those that bear on salvation. You cannot state your belief in such a Christ except by a theology. Your experience of Him must be couched in the forms of a definite historic religion. Yet our relation to Him is not historic assent or ideal interest; it is a positive personal relation of moral communion, power, and victory in the Holy Ghost. The only contemporary Christ is not a Christ restored to history merely, but a Christ returned to heaven. Who was it that in the first age saved Christianity for the future? Who was it that was the mediator of the historic Christ to the generations that followed Christ, and thus to the whole of Christian posterity? Was it not the great theological believer and apostle, Paul, for whom Christ was not simply a character but the Gospel, not a product of God but an act of God, nay God in action? It is such great Gospellers, not the historians, that are the mediators of our spiritual future. I call Paul the fifth Evangelist, and we ought to call him the first in point of time and of value both. To the Church he is the greatest of all—however attractive the synoptical figure alone may be to a humanist democracy, or to a religionist rather than a faithful Church. The Synoptic Gospels alone would never have made Christendom. Paul is the evangelist of the Gospel within the Gospels, and he made one of them, the Fourth Gospel, possible. Do not entertain the suggestion, the myth, that Paul made the pure Gospel of Jesus turbid with his floating Judaic theologoumena. Did Paul, the practical founder of the Church whose foundation is Christ, make a fundamental mistake about the genius of Christ's Gospel and the atoning nature of reigning grace?

VII

Let me place this in conjunction with our own Church genius. On what do we Congregationalists rest the position of the ministry in the Church? How do we justify the Church's right to invite its own minister? On this very principle—that the Church has the touchstone in its evangelical experience for any preacher who comes with the authority of the Gospel. We do not accept him on the certificate of his college, or the word of his fellow-ministers (far less on the choice of a prime minister), but on our own inward testimony that he finds us, but finds us as the Gospel did—which found us lost and left us saved. Those unfound by the Gospel have, in our theory, no strict right in his choice—none to decide it, however, they may be consulted in courtesy or convenience. He is the choice, not of men who like Christianity, or admire Christ, but of men whom the real positive Christian Gospel has already found and saved, and made confessors of Christ. It is not simply that the preacher finds *us*, touches *us*, reaches our best selves. That makes man the standard instead of the Gospel. It is that he finds our evangelical, our redeemed, selves. He re-echoes what first found us so. You hear people say, "I will vote for that man; he has done me good; I know he has—as I know when I have had a good meal." That is sheer individual subjectivism. It is the mistake so many Churches make to-day; and it is the cause of the deadly restlessness that sets in, and the impatience, when the personal freshness has worn off a preacher who is not a scribe instructed in the old novelties of the Bible and its rich Gospel. Who and what are you whom the preacher has satisfied? What has he satisfied? By what have you tested him? He appeals to your experience—of what? Of your own better self or of the Gospel? You would choose him for your minister; would Christ for His apostle? Is he for you a minister of the Gospel, or of your ideals, tastes, affections, and idiosyncrasies? Of the mighty objective Gospel, or of your subjective piety and your age's humane sentiments? I ask, Who you are? Are you one who has really tasted the Gospel of God's grace to you a sinner? Are you able to say, "This is indeed an apostle of the Cross, a minister of Grace, an expert in the Gospel, and a distributor of the Bread of Life; it grows in his hands"? Or do you say, like so many, "This is a man, a real man, an able man, a cultured man, a genial man, a tender man, a children's man, a bold man, a gentleman; this is my man"? Very gratifying to be sure, especially to the happy favourite. But not the main test for a minister of the Gospel—only the test for a preacher or teacher of a religious society, which is a very different thing. Or may be only the test for the minister of a set within the Church, which is nothing at all. We face a world where wickedness is thorough enough. And we face it with a full salvation, costly but free. What have we to do with seraphic smatterers in the Gospel or the soul?

I do not mean anything so foolish as that the two things must be parted—the grace of God and grace with man. I mean only that it is the former that makes the minister, not the latter. It is the Gospel and not the style, the power and not the charm. I mean that the one must always serve the other; that favour with men shall always wait upon fidelity to the Gospel; that this and not that shall be the decisive thing in a call—with all the accomplishment, charm, and effect that grace can breed in the preacher's personality. As it is, the preacher may minister to men's moods rather than their life. All Christians, and especially preachers, fall into two classes—those to whom their Christianity is a temperament, and those to whom it is a life. And the temperament may betray the Gospel. The graces of the preacher's word may muffle the word of God's grace.

VIII

But how, indeed, can our people test a minister of the Gospel? Do they read their Bibles? (I speak very generally.) Have they a first-hand acquaintance with the book of the Gospel, as the men had who founded Congregationalism, and founded it not on the democratic principle but on the evangelical? A Church whose members do not use the Bible as their constant and supreme means of grace has lost the Congregational basis and right, which is evangelical or nothing. Such communities may have a democratic right. As they support the preacher they should choose his tune. (But there, you see—"Choose his tune," not, "Recognize his Gospel." We do not choose that—we have to accept its choice of us.) Such a Church may be as democratic, bustling, and benevolent as you please, but it has no evangelical right. It has no right based on the Gospel. It may choose its orator, or its president in that way, not its minister. For the Gospel (I keep saying) did not come to make democratic clubs, but to make Churches of men made by it and living on it daily and deeply. Democracy so far has been called a moral failure. And if so, it can only be saved by a Church whose genius is something very different, which owns in its holy Gospel a moral authority outside itself, or its sympathies, affinities, and aspirations—an authority which is really in command of life, and not an outlying interest. It is one thing to use religion to sustain or soothe the best in human life. A society may be formed to do that, but it is not a Church. Call it a fraternity, a coterie, or what you will, it is all subjective and finally feeble. But it is another thing to use human life for the Gospel, to submit all our experiences to that outward authority, to trust it rather to redeem our worst than to develop our best, to make the Gospel of God's grace our one goal and glory, to let it create a new life rather than to patch an old lapse. Such a Gospel makes its own society. And that is a true Church, the Church we need most; and it has a Church's right and duty of recognizing as minister the man who is in the Apostolic succession, and has the Gospel note, and not the man who is the most social, energetic, cultivated, or popular. When I began to preach the chief test of a minister was orthodoxy. And I had the honour to suffer something alongside those who have changed that. But now the test is agreeableness of person and message; and about that I am not happy. It is the sympathetic note, whatever the nature of the man's word might be, or however he might play fast and loose with the Word of God. Much welcome preaching may be simply reckless with the Bible if the phrase of a text suit some topic. Well, if there were no other choice I would rather go back to the old test. For it judged the man by the message and not the message by the man. Orthodoxy did give you a standard outside the moods and tastes, whether of individuals or of groups. It did give you an objective Divine rock upon which to build a Church instead of subjective human sand. It did force you back on your own Bible, even if it did not read every part aright. But we are not shut up to that reactionary alternative. There is a test of an objective kind for those who qualify themselves to apply it. It is this test and authority of the Gospel, the evangelical test, the prolongation into the pulpit, not only of the spiritual *note* of the New Testament but of its positive saving mighty *word*, answered and verified in the responsible and scriptural experience of the true members of the Church.

Responsible! Remember always, please, that I speak of a Church and its minister, not of a mission and its leader. I would deprecate the erasure of the difference, the turning of every Church into no more than a mission station, or saying that the Church has no other than a missionary or evangelizing function. Missions are bound to suffer if that idea prevail. It makes them suffer now; for the root reason of the difficulties of missions is that the Churches are doing more justice to the Kingdom than to the cross. I wish we would take our missionary difficulties more seriously. You cannot spread the Kingdom by preaching the Kingdom. Christ Himself failed with that. It sacrifices the intensive work of the Church to its extensive. It externalizes and finally secularizes. It turns preaching into a propagand only. It does not stoke the fires that make the train go. Missionary methods are something *per se*, where Christianity is in direct contact with the paganism of Society at home or abroad. And I rejoice that in Home Missions they are making a fresh appeal to our imagination. But in a settled Church (I hope there will be no insults to the great idea) it is different. Missions are a prime function of a Church; but they are not the Church itself. It is the experience, the faith of a Church that the pastor should first stir, and feed, and make missionary.

IX

Something has come between us and our Gospel. In some quarters it is the Bible. There has been such a thing as Bibliolatry. There is such a thing as Biblicism at the cost of the Spirit. Men become positive about Bible facts and views instead of about the Bible word of grace. Elsewhere it is the Church that has cast the shadow. Elsewhere it is the ministry. Elsewhere it is a sect, based perhaps on a single doctrine. Elsewhere it is the State. Elsewhere it is Humanity. Some forms of social service obscure the Gospel within our Churches. Elsewhere it is some special type of religion made supreme. It is a cosy family piety, or a coterie piety, or a happy young people's piety, or a tasty, literary, liberal piety. It may be the very freedom of thought for which so many Christians have worked, suffered, and died. Our liberal Christianity may come in the way of a positive Gospel. There are circles where each of these is in the way of the classic Gospel. There is not one of the blessings sown by the Gospel that has not sprung up and choked it. Its three great products—the Church, the Ministry, the Bible—have all threatened its life at some time and in some way. They each tend to do it still if we cease to live directly on the Gospel and if we put any of its products in its place. Nay, is it not possible to let Jesus come between us and the Gospel? Is it not done from two sides—by those who treat Him as a moral paragon, and by those who treat Him as a miraculous prodigy? Is it not done by the man who admires His character and teaching but will have nothing of a Redemption, abjures an Atonement, reduces sin to ignorance, guilt to imperfection, forgiveness to amnesty, and the fatherhood to patriarchal kindness? And is it not done at the other extreme by the man who stakes the whole value of Jesus on His earthly omniscience, and perils the whole Gospel on the Davidic authorship of a Psalm that Jesus used? Is that not letting a certain conception of Christ come between us and His Gospel? Is it not interpreting the Gospel by the Bible instead of the Bible by the Gospel?

The very Christianity in which we find our salvation needs to be saved. It is the constant work of the Holy Spirit to save for the Gospel what comes down to our day as saving truth. It is only by constant and intelligent effort that we keep our religion real, and translate the great tradition into the original experience of our soul and age. It is so much easier to imitate those who have felt its inner power than to reproduce it in ourselves. But nothing else saves salvation. On the voyage of the Church we need daily to "take the sun." Experience of the Gospel, moral, personal, daily, is the only fidelity to the Gospel, and its only guarantee against decadence. I repeat that in this respect the Bible, treated as a palladium, may become a peril like the other products of the Gospel—the Church, the creeds, and the ministry. It does not matter how imposing or beneficent any of these products of the Gospel may be, we pay too dear for it if we have it at the cost of our evangelical experience. Theology, Churchmanship, Philanthropy—every one of them men may make, men have made, men do make, enemies of the cross of Christ, and clouds upon His Gospel.

Each of these great products must be borne back upon their Gospel to be quickened and saved by its touch. It was this that the Reformers did. They depreciated neither Bible,

Church, nor ministry. But they revised them all, and they reconstituted them all by the Bible's Gospel. Such is always the work of the Holy Spirit—to elicit new power and new meaning from Christ, His cross, His work. It is to urge us back ever anew upon the cross as the source where the Spirit issues which created Christendom, and continually regenerates Christendom. The Spirit of Christ is the Spirit of Messiah, of deliverance, of Gospel. The witness of the Spirit is Christ's perpetual interpretation of His own work as Gospel. It lights the Bible, it leads the Church, it anoints the ministry, and all by a constant rejuvenation of the Gospel and of its power to create, criticize, and create anew. The holiness of the cross was in its critical judgment no less than in its creative grace.

X

If we take a large enough view of our position and its weakness, is it not something like this? As a whole we have never really faced the spiritual situation created by the collapse of Biblical infallibility for communities that had long repudiated the final authority of the Church. And it is more essential that this situation should be faced than that we should come to terms with the working-class, or any class, about the social question. The relation of the Church to spiritual thought, to culture in that sense, is even more important than its relation to labour. It is more necessary that we should face the spiritual situation than the social, even for the sake of doing anything for the social that shall be of decisive worth. The writers in *Lux Mundi*, for instance, were not in our predicament. They almost seemed to welcome the results of criticism on the New Testament no less than the Old, as forcing people anew on the authority of their Church. What, then, is left for us to do who cannot accept the old authority either of the Church or the Bible?

What is left for us but to go back to our Bible, and rediscover what the Bible goes back on? What have we but the glorious refuge of the Gospel of Grace, of Christ's moral redemption, with its appeal to the everlasting conscience, its sole solution of man's moral problem and moral blight, and its restoration of holiness to the altar of the Church and the throne of the moral world? We, too, must thank God for the criticism that forces us back past the Church of Grace and through the Bible to the historic Gospel of Grace.

We should seek a settlement to satisfy the just claims on each side. We ought, on the one hand, to meet those who sympathize with Biblical criticism with something else than a reckless *non possumus*. And we ought, on the other hand, to meet with something else than the charge of obscurantism those whose love and knowledge of the Bible is uncritical. There are those yonder to whom it is but a great historic record or the crown of religious literature; and there are those here to whom it is the greatest of all the means of grace. No solution is complete which does not give both their due. One would do a good deal to recognize the value to the Bible of the schools and geniuses of scholarship that have brought new, brilliant, and fruitful methods to bear on it. And one would give more to restore the Bible to the place it had in the personal piety of our fathers.

XI

What is the reality we are resting on—actually and practically I mean, not in the theory of the thing? Use an effort of imagination. Deduct, if your thought can, all that you are doing, all the Churches are doing, in the way of consolation to the harassed soul, of stimulus to the aspiring soul, or of social reform for the oppressed soul. Ask yourself what would be left to our Churches if these functions were detached, or thrown into the background which they occupy in the Bible. Are they the elements which submerge all else in the Bible? They do not cover the whole of the Christian programme, do they? Well, when you discount them in thought from our Churches to-day what have you left? Have you the evangelizing, converting, redeeming power over the world's soul left which fills the foreground of the Bible? If you denied yourself, for a time and as an experiment, those subjects and efforts, what would be left you to preach? Would the reality go out of your religion if you thought away its soothing, aspiring, or philanthropic effects? What would remain if you thought away everything that a fine Unitarian would preach equally well? Would you still have a Gospel? If you deducted from our preaching the sympathetic element (which God forbid!), would you be left with the moral-evangelical element as a living stock to raise sympathies more fresh and Christian still? Is there not an order of reality deeper than any we sound in the ministrations of comfort, kindling, or service? Is there not behind it all the reality of the moral soul, of the guilty conscience, of the world lying in wickedness, of the kingdom of evil? Is it not the power which deals with this that is the most real and the most needed of all? Is it not the Gospel of judging, redeeming grace, and of costly moral peace with God for the soul and for Society?

How far is that left with us, behind all those interests and energies I have named? Is it not a power lacking in many of our favourite forms of piety? Which is it that the world needs most—sympathy or salvation? Is it pity or mercy? Is it stimulus or forgiveness? Is it moral help or moral reconstruction for the soul? And which are we offering in chief? We read eagerly in the book of the heart and the age, but do we read more (as we should do) in the book of the Word?

Do we keep our sympathies in the key of the Bible, in the proportion and perspective of faith? Do we keep them fed by an experienced redemption? All sanctification is but the working out of a central redemption. It is the growth of our faith in forgiveness and all it implies. But does the reconciliation, the sweetness, in our piety keep going back to the atoning redemption and drawing moral power from that root? Or are we not trying to get the spirit by going round the Bible and the Cross instead of through them? When we do offer the age something out of the Bible, do we get to reality with it, to the deep reality in God and the last reality in man? Do we work with that which arrests the first-rate minds, which searches man to his tragic foundation, and secures his eternal destiny once and for ever? You must work with that deep word, powerful and not merely forcible, of searching sanctity as well as pervasive sympathy. You cannot rest a real religion on a social programme, or an impressionist effect, upon interests which are chiefly contemporary, or sermons which are genial literature. You must have a moral basis, a moral message, and a moral effect, as morality is required by a guilty world and a helpless conscience, before a broken law, an affronted love, and an angry God. It is not a world out of joint that makes our problem, but the shipwrecked soul in it. It is Hamlet, not his world, that is wrong. It is not the contradictions of life, and its anomalies, that make the real trouble, but the unfaith, the falsity of those who live. It is the soul's own civil war, the rebellion of man-soul, its sullen severance from God, its ostrich hope of escaping His law, its silly notions of making it up with Him, its hate and dread of Him, its sin, and the triviality of its sense of sin. What we need is not new truth, new ideas, new theology. What can any truth, new or old, do for sin? Sin is more than untruth, more than ignorance. What can ideas or theologies do for my wickedness? The truth about even God never convicted of sin. It was the coming of God. Christianity does not peddle ideas; it does things. Reality lies in action, and Christ has done the deed of history. What we need is new power, new reality and a new kind of it, a regeneration not a reform, a holy, costly Saviour, and not a blessed saint. What we need most is neither to feel nor to act differently, but power to be different, to be a new creature, and live in a new world. And our new world is not like America—just the other side of the old. It is another order of things, values, and powers in the cross. Well, are our Churches making the new man, or are they simply refurbishing the old man? Can the Gospel we ply make the new man? Would he not be a poor thing often if it could? Are we making our Bible yield the Gospel that can? I heard a sermon some time ago on "Blessed are they that hunger and thirst after righteousness, for they shall be filled," and all the stress was laid on the nobility of such hunger; not a word was said about the Gospel of sure and certain satisfaction in which alone the blessedness lies. I have heard other sermons in the same vein. That is quite typical of the way the Bible is used to-day, to exhibit the worth of human nature on its unworldly side rather than to carry home the blessedness of the man to whom the Lord imputeth not his guilt. It is interesting and honoured for something else than the Gospel—for its human dignity, depth, beauty, or tenderness, only not for the thing that gave it its being, its task, and its power. The very Bible is captured and made to grind in the mill of that subjectivity which is the blight upon our modern religion.

XII

The age asks many things from the Church which flit through the public mind only to be quickly forgotten. But one thing it needs whether it has wit to ask for it or not. And this supreme thing is not sympathy. The hour's great need is objective footing—reality; and it is a hopeful thing that in many quarters men are coming to ask for reality quite as much as for sympathy. We do impress the public with our sympathy. The Churches, the preachers, the hospitals, and all the charities are in a holy alliance for that. But we do not impress the public with our reality or authority. We lack the note of power, penetration, and mastery. We lack a fulcrum. We do not make our realities more impressive and effectual with the world than its own. The mediaeval Church did. That is why some serious minds wish to drag us back to it. The Roman Church largely does still. Do you think you would get grown and able men to submit to the confessional but for the fear of what the Church succeeds in making good—a very real hell, and a very real power to keep people out of it? And there is something worse than not stamping our realities upon the world. We do not convey the impression to it, on the whole, that our realities are supremely real to ourselves. And why? Because we are not in moral earnest with the Gospel for our age, as Christ was, as Paul was, as the Bible is. In some ways we are more in earnest with our age than with our Gospel for it.

I pray you do not be impatient when I speak so much of reality. And do not suspect a flavour of philosophy instead of contact with facts. Do not take my arm and lead me away to the dwellings of the pound-a-weeks and the nothing-a-weeks and tell me if I want realities to consider there. Long ago I was there, and worked there, and considered there, and have been considering ever since. The squalors and miseries of life are not its realities. They are its actualities. They would break every feeling heart that is not stayed upon life's realities from elsewhere. And they would submerge every society that cares nothing for the reality it touches in God and His Gospel alone. Society is past saving by the philanthropists. It needs mighty evangelists. It is in our morals and not in our miseries that we confront the great realities of the world. It is an age's moral poverty that faces us, and something like the bankruptcy of the old spiritual house.

XIII

The age's need for the secure, supreme, and objective reality of a spiritual world can only be met by the way of the holy Gospel to the actual historical conscience. What cries to be done is to make the spiritual world a moral reality. To do that we must present it as an atoning Gospel adjusted to our peculiar moral extremity. We shall never get what we want by coquetting with the higher physics, nor by psychical research, nor by theosophic religion, nor by diluted Hegel, nor by mystical, fanciful, sermonic, and unhistoric treatment of the Bible. We can get it only by the moral power and effect of a historic Gospel, and one that draws us from the belly of hell. That abyss is real enough to us. And our certainty, our true reality, stands in our redemption from it. Morality, social or private, can only be secured by holiness; and holiness in such a world can only be secured by redemption. We shall never be real or holy by trying to be either, but only by trusting and loving the Most Holy and Real. The age's soul can only find its forwandered self by trust toward a God forgiving and saving it on the scale of all history in the hell-harrowing, heaven-scaling Cross of Christ. The spiritual authority of the long future rests where rests the effectual power to judge, forgive, and redeem the evil conscience. And this is true whether what we feel most is sin or sympathy. The sense of sin may be low, but its reality and its action are all the more fatal. The final reality of life is in its tragic conflict of good and evil, God and sin. It lies in the practical region, not in the ideal; and in the region of the practical conscience paralysed by its own failure, schism, and wickedness. Every cultured and prosperous age tends to lose sight of this. Every humane age does. It loses practical sense of the solemn centrality of this issue, even while it makes and likes sermons about it. It ceases to realize the awfulness of wickedness and the amount of it, and, therefore, of its cure. It extenuates, it even pooh-poohs the radical evil in human nature, and the diabolical element in the soul. We become victimized by what may be called the pink pieties, the poetry of the pulpit, or the wan sanctity of the coterie. People live so decently and feebly that they do not believe that it is possible to hate God. They declare that no man who really recognizes the Divine can reject and hate it; if any do so it is in ignorance or misapprehension. But those who hold such a happy faith in human nature hold it in ignorance. They may be of somewhat bloodless nature, or of sheltered and lady-like experience. There is plenty in history and in society to upset their optimism. There is more still in the death of Christ. The purest, deepest, humanest, holiest being the world ever saw it harried out of it. And would it not do it again? We not only have egoism perfectly unscrupulous in pursuing its object, but egoism itself passes beyond itself into a malign hatred, envy, and *Schadenfreude*, even when its own person or objects are not interfered with. There are those who find a joy in defiling, degrading, and defying the holiest and the best. There is wickedness of the diabolic sort, love of evil as evil, and sin against the Holy Ghost. All that has ever been condensed into our conception of a devil exists in human nature as a devilish element. And to cope with that the last reality has to be drawn upon. It is in the region of that conflict, and there alone, that we touch the deepest foundation of things, in the region of radical evil. And that is the region of Christ's cross, Christ's conflict with the last enemy, Christ's victory by absolute holiness—the region of the Gospel. Nothing we experience can secure us on the rock of spiritual reality, or fix us on the last foundation of being, till we experience the Gospel as God's utmost with man's worst, the Gospel of Redemption by gracious judgment. We are saved hardly. You cannot realize the greatness of Christ without realizing the might of Antichrist, rising as we draw to the latter days. True spirituality is not the highest stage of the blossoming world, but it is the world beaten, broken, and led captive. It stands not on the world's development, but on a break with the world, the inroad of a new life in a new kind. A Christ that differs from the rest of men only in saintly degree and not in redeeming kind is not the Christ of the New Testament nor of a Gospel Church. The Gospel is not the fatherhood, but the redeeming fatherhood. Nor is faith simple sonship, but the sonship of adoption and grace. It is not the imitation of Christ, but the appropriation of Him. These old metaphors, like adoption, mark what is missing in the new piety and the most modern Church.

XIV

It would be easy to set a whole vicinity by the ears with gratuitous discourses on the Higher Criticism—for or against—but it is not easy to make religious men rend their hearts before the High and Holy Critic, whose judgment is at the doors and His Gospel very nigh within. Do we realize what a fierce critic Christ was of the earnest religion of His day—so earnest that these Pharisees would readily have died for it? He and they were alike earnest there. But no earnestness in their religion excused the want of moral insight into Him. Now the best men on earth I believe to be in the ministry, the men on whom God's eye rests as His ownest own amid the care, sin, and din of the world. Certainly the dearest men to me are there. I love you brethren, and I tell you so. But how many of those who preach in all the Churches are *mighty* in the Scriptures after His way—straight and sure in getting at their objective core and moral word?

How few grasp the Bible historically, and interpret it from that start to the need created by history for their age! How many lack that note of reality which the age's heart craves to meet and leaps to find! We are not insincere. I do not mean that. Hypocrisy has been well scourged out of us. But we are unreal—some knowing it, some not. We are unreal, sentimental and impressionist—we are in danger of being histrionic, with our Gospel. We handle the eternities, yet we cannot go to the bottom of things. Our Churches often seem to have more faith in what can be done by the skilful preacher than by his Gospel. We do not dwell beside the remorseless reality of God in His saving work, and so we do not reach with the final and conquering word the core of man and his need. We look on the world and say, "Ah! the pity of it." We do not delve in our own hearts, as Matthew Arnold complained, and say, "Oh! the curse of it." In a word, we do not grasp the moral tragedy of the race's suicide, and we do not grasp the Gospel. The very word Gospel may become a piece of pious slang. We do not betray enough of the manner of people who are habitually under authority to it, who are held by it, crushed and born again by it, people who are broken to pieces and made again from the dust, people who are shut for ever from the old Eden, faced with turning flaming swords, and forced by pursuing grace through a dreadful world to a new heaven and earth wherein dwelleth holiness. So much of our religious teaching betrays no sign that the speaker has descended into hell, been near the everlasting burnings, or been plucked from the awful pit. He has risen with Christ—what right have we to deny it?—but it is out of a shallow grave, with no deepness of earth, with no huge millstone to roll away. It is the thin Gospel of a Bible either neglected or feebly conventionalized. We hear talk of repentance as if it were at best but sincere regret, and of confession as if it were mere apology. We confess fluently such things as we can name in public; we may even do it in a way that increases the public sense of our virtue; and we seem incapable of the unspeakable agony and mortal shame. We sleep and dream through Gethsemane. And if we rise above earth it is often but glibly, and we do not come bemazed to the third heaven, where we see things we may not speak. We grow our souls for exportation; and we may exploit our secret communion with God more than we bear witness of the God and Gospel that have given us that reconciliation. We do not experience that action of the Gospel, or we do not prolong the tradition of those who did. When we soothe and comfort we do not do it as men who once touched the central fires and carry scars. We tune down so much. The new creation appears but as fresh growth. God becomes the spirit of a cosmic world. Providence becomes the action of the moral order, or the principle of spiritual evolution. The soul is our consciousness, with the risk of ceasing when that does. Heaven is a vague future. Resurrection means no more than going on living at a fresh height. The Kingdom of God is the empire of goodness and love. Prayer becomes aspiration and meditation, and it ceases to be prevailing with God. Sacraments become mere memorials or mere symbols, which, like poor preachers, speak but effect nothing. And when I say *we*, I do not mean that our Churches have fallen to this at every point. But it is certainly the tone of that fringe of the world which just comes up to the Church and touches it. And its effect has passed into the Churches in no small degree, especially through the favourite reading of the half-cultured.

One reads somnambulant sermons about coming into tune with the infinite, about cultivating the presence of God, about pausing in life to hear the melodies of the everlasting chime, and all the rest of the romance of piety breathed beneath the moon in the green and pleasant glades of devotion—all without a hint of the classic redemption, or even of the Christ, whereby alone we have access to any of the rich quietives of faith. The preacher has glimpses of the paradise, but no sense of the purgatorio. He has the language but not the accent of that far heavenly country. Oh! but we want men who have been there and been naturalized there. We want more than romantic and temperamental piety. We want the accent of the Holy Ghost, learned with a new life at its classic capital—the cross. We want something more than a lovely Gospel with the fine austerity of a cloistered ethic. I do not wonder that the literary people react from self-conscious Galahad, sure and vain of his own purity, and turn to welcome the smell of the good brown earth. So also our virile sinfulness turns from the criticisms of fastidious religion to the *blood* of Christ and the cost at which we are scarcely saved. It was not Galahad or Arthur that drew Christ from heaven. It was a Lancelot race. It was a tragic issue of man's passion that called out the glory of Christ. It is a most tragic world, this, for those who see to the bottom of it and leave us their witness to its confusion, as Shakespeare did in *Hamlet*, *Lear*, and even *The Tempest*. He had to leave it there, stated in pathetic majesty but unreconciled. But what that mighty age could not do in Shakespeare it did in its Puritans. They had found a reconcilement which belonged to a larger world than Shakespeare's, and a deeper vision than that of solemn tragedy. For their life was no tragedy, but a redemption going beneath the foundations of the world. It was a redemption that had gone through tragedy and come out at the other side, in a solemn music and Divine comedy. They were more than Shakespearian; they were Dantesque. They had realized more than the fate of sin; they had measured its guilt. They knew what it cost man in happiness; but they knew still more what it cost God in the Cross. They knew the tragedy of life which makes man man; but still more they knew the redemption which makes God God.

XV

Let us try to see things in a large context, in a deep and solemn world. Let us be less anxious to have the verdict of the man in the street (or, as the Bible has it, "the wayfaring man though a fool"). Let us covet more of the distinction which is inseparable from a spiritual authority. It is easy to have vigour without distinction, simplicity without the subtlety of the Holy Ghost. The democracy which is our problem loves vigour and simplicity, but these alone will not save it. Lusty force and elemental sympathies, grandiose pictures and the touch of the child—these will always fetch the public, but they will not save it. And they are not enough to seize, hold, and guide a whole old nation with a great historic civilization. Without a theology we cannot appeal to the scientific imagination, without an authority we cannot move the moral imagination. With an appeal only to the tender imagination, or to none, the end is sentimentalism and then decadence. And we shall not be saved from that morass merely by mindless preoccupation with the hour's moralities or the home's affections. The heart itself craves more than that; and if we give it no more, our audiences will become like a great roomful of people listening to bad music and false pathos given with an affectation of dainty execution and fine art; listening and making believe to like it, when their true hearts are waiting to be stormed by a fiery old ballad or captured by one full of pathos too deep for tears. I do not say we need a revived public interest in theology as the Queen of Culture. If I said that I suppose I should be called a pedant. But we do need the handling of all issues in the spirit of men who have the range and type of mind congenial to theology. Oh, for a blast of that dread horn which Gladstone used to wind!

Let us withdraw some attention from press and platform

questions to the ultimate questions that solve the rest. Let us screw to a sticking-point our national cowardice in spiritual matters, so faithfully reflected in the theological timidity of the national Church. Let us ask ourselves where we really stand. Let us try to read our problems on a European, an Ecumenical scale. Let us free ourselves from bondage to the talk of the conventicle, the ethic of the conventicle, the little world of it. (And I call no Church a conventicle, however small, which has a true sense of its place in the great Church which God builds and not man.) Let us think in an atmosphere other than the mass meeting or the journal. Let us avoid the hypocrisy of large words with small ideas or none. Let us gain the habit of asking where our new positions lead us. Let us fear to move about in worlds not realized. Let us, for instance, ask, in a responsible way, every time we question the authority of the Bible on a certain point, what we have done, what we are doing, to secure men in the obedience of some final unquestionable authority. What have our people acquired to take the place of an infallible Bible for the Gospel and for the world? What have we given them? It is so easy to say, I no longer believe in this or that my fathers taught me. And it seems broad and intelligent. And the young man in the pew may talk like that going up in the train. But the man in the pulpit should have got beyond that blurting form of honesty. He has a special responsibility. He has a duty of honest reserve which does not lie on the pew. Honesty for him does not mean speaking out so much as thinking out. It is not honest for the public leader to speak out on the gravest matters without thinking out. It is better to think out to a wrong conclusion than to be content with conclusions which are not thought out at all, but merely ejaculated. Much public speech on religion is ejaculation. It is made up of interjections without any conjunctions. The most logical sermon, if it be inspired only by a recent book, or an article gulped from a current journal, is in the nature of an interjection. It is ejaculated, as I say. It has no context in the man's mind. You tell the public, for instance, you do not believe in a personal devil. Very well. You do not forfeit your place in an evangelical Church for that. Satan is not even in the Athanasian Creed. But before you said it did you think it out? The New Testament certainly has that belief. Your people find it there. Were they protected in advance from the confusion thus created? Had they had explained to them the precise place of the Bible as an objective authority, or, failing the Bible, were they secured in some other? Besides, there is no doubt Christ held that belief. And it is on a totally different footing from His views about the date of a Psalm. For He came directly to cope with evil at its fountain-head; and He did not come to settle Old Testament scholarship in advance. Have you worked out the relation of your denial to the work of Christ, and its effect on His moral authority? Have you asked yourself what follows if He did not know the real nature of His great antagonist in a world-conflict? I am not settling the question, I am only indicating its dimensions. And do not tell me here that people do not want theology. It is not a question of theology, nor of popular appetite. It is a question of mental honesty, thoroughness, and cohesion.

Or, again, a man preaches that the difference between Christ and men was one of degree only, not of kind. Well, I am less sure than in the other instance about the right of such teaching in a Church of the Gospel. Christ as a perfect Man moving to God is no authority for our faith, as He is no object of our worship; He is so only as redeeming God moving to man. That is His place in any Church of His Gospel. Has the measure of such a statement been taken, the statement that Christ differs from other men but in degree? Does it not give up the heart of the Gospel and the Church's reason for being? Or do we measure the parallel statement that the fatherhood of God is but our best human fatherhood infinitely magnified? Has it been asked what becomes of the grace of God if that be so?

Are statements of that tremendous kind not sometimes made hastily, crudely, by men who have not been trained to handle them, to measure their intrinsic gravity, and gauge their collateral effects upon other beliefs and on the public? You say the truth must be spoken without regard to consequences. Certainly without regard to consequences to yourself from men's favour or dislike. But surely not without regard to the implications of the position for the whole coherent field of faith and for the final Kingdom. The man who speaks so is too casual, too irresponsible.

I know that the people we speak to will, in many cases, discourage a cautious treatment of final questions, or the treatment of all questions in a final way. But if we preach only what our people encourage we may gain the public, but sell our Gospel, and lose our soul. Our Gospel is not what the people encourage but what encourages the people, steadies the people, and on occasion respectfully withstands the people. And if you compel them to face questions which make them complain that you are over their heads, meet them with the reply, "Lift up your heads." No man has any business to be obscure. But no man ought to avoid the last and greatest issues simply because he is thought so by the mass of the public and its caterers who do not sound the Gospel on which it is his business to wait continually. Those who take in earnest an infinite Gospel to such a world, are always obscure to those who do not. There is nothing more obscure to common sense, with its dullness to the great world powers, than the personal experience of faith which believes in present grace, real judgment, and final good amid a world that lies in wickedness.

XVI

No amount of social compunction or effort will give the Church power to annul its past neglect, and become the Saviour of Society, except as it is itself saved by the Gospel and mastered by its grace. It is unsaved to an extent it is far from realizing—and almost as far at its left as at its right. Neither the repentance of the orthodox nor the works of the liberal can win the salvation which is a pure gift of grace. We know that that is so for individuals. But we are not so sure that it is so with Churches. But so it is. It is a case of re-establishing in our very midst the grace of God as life's active ethical power, moving it to life's real centre, and taking all our practical bearings from it anew. The Church may carry its sympathies much farther than it has done. It may trawl the slums. It may win the confidence of the working-class in a quite new way. It may cover Asia and Africa with missions. And at home it may assimilate the results of all culture. We may even thrill at Christ's name, purify the idea of God, press a Christian view of society and conduct, vindicate the historic Jesus and His scheme of life. We may do all that and more, and yet miss the life of grace. But if we do not grasp the old Gospel of grace as our own central experience, it will mean final failure. We shall lose heart and power. The Church's victory can only be by way of its moral authority, which is grace. not love; mercy, and not pity. The morality of pity has no imperative. It is in the Gospel of grace alone that we possess the moral charter and the moral power which have the *entrée* to man's last recesses, the reversion of the last days, and the promise of the ends of the earth.

Why, for instance, has Protestant Christianity been unable to do more against a Church so pagan in its genius as Rome; and especially against a Rome that has fallen from even its first estate, and accepted its modern salvation from the

Jesuits? Why does Protestantism not rule Europe at least? Why but because its orthodoxy retains so much that is more Catholic than Christian; because its humanism becomes naturalist, its liberty mere liberalism, and its duty secular; because its well-doing becomes so conventional and even trivial—in a word, because it has failed to realize its own Gospel as singly and thoroughly as its opponent has realized the Church? It is never Protestantism that will vanquish Rome and save Society from it. No mere Church will ever vanquish that Church. None will ever take the Church idea more in earnest, or adjust it more skilfully to organized civilization. In America, for instance, will any Church be able to provide such a refuge as Rome may do by a wise policy for those who are sick of the mammonism and individualism that gnaw at the vitals of democracy there? It is no rival Church or theology, as such, that will conquer what we would see conquered in Catholicism. Do you think it will be your Free Church principles, or your Free Church organization, that will cope with Anglicanism? No, it must be done by the Gospel, by your principles only as corollaries of the Gospel. It is a victory that nothing but a Gospel-mastered Church can win. It is an evangelical revival, in the greatest, strangest sense of the words, that all the greatest humanest causes need. Protestantism may rock to and fro indefinitely, locked in the great wrestle with Catholicism, but fail to throw it to the ground. Only the Gospel will succeed in that. For the two cannot live in the same house. The grace of the Gospel and the grace of that Church are two hostile things. But do not be deceived. This might of the Gospel will change Protestantism almost as much as Catholicism, and our liberal, humane, and attractive Protestantism as much as the hard old orthodoxy.

So, if we are not wasting our force, we are at least preparing for ourselves a disappointment in every effort to christianize Society, so long as we pursue it on lines that are merely socialist, humane, or based on that natural and unconscious Christianity which is too often the liberal note. Our Churches are at the parting of the ways. Owing to the change in our view of the Bible, it is a choice between sympathy and authority. We have begun to drop the note of authority—to drop it because we have lost it with an infallible book—and we are adopting a note which is almost entirely that of sympathy. Well, for final purposes it is a wrong choice. And we are taking it partly because it is half right, partly because about the other half we are unsure, partly because it is easier. (Let me say in passing that when I speak of sympathy I am speaking of a note of a Church, I am not speaking of the tone of individuals, any more than when I mention authority I mean an authoritative manner in preachers.) Anglicanism takes the note of authority with the people, and has but little sympathy. It abuses the idea of the supernatural. The Free Churches take the note of sympathy, with little authority. They tend to lose the idea of the supernatural. Both extremes are wrong and sterile. The Church of the future must have the note of sympathetic authority. This is especially necessary for dealing with young men. Without it their Christian endeavours may only unsex them. But the authority must be no less unmistakable than the sympathy, however we regain it. We are not prepared to replace any form of Catholicism till we reach it. The key and command of human nature is in the supernatural; and the most supernatural thing in the world is God's redeeming grace. What we need is not less sympathy with people, but more sympathy with powers like that. It is our attitude to that Gospel that will decide our fate; and the prime attitude to the Gospel is not sympathy but obedience. We do not sympathize with our Saviour, we worship Him. The Gospel is not a humanity but an authority, and the only one which guarantees the human fraternity of the world. We must give ourselves with all our might to recover for our Churches the faith which joys more in the experience of redeeming grace than in all the victories of reform. "Restore to me the joy of Thy salvation." A social Gospel will only turn our Churches into clubs and our religion into hearty bustle, unless it flow from a new reality of faith among us. And that again can only flow from a new grasp of Christ's grace which may bewilder orthodox and liberal alike, Churchman and Humanist. It will seem great and good to those alone who live in their Bible, but only breathe in the free and moving world.

XVII

The peril of the hour is a religious subjectiveness which is gliding down into a religious decadence for want of an objective authority and an external standard on which to climb. In Protestantism we have but the one standard of grace for theology and for religion. What tells on the one tells on the other. If our type of belief lose its central authority our true type of piety falls with it. Our Christianity is often little more than Christian culture or Christian civilization, or a Christian ideal, or a Christian scheme. It is Christian enthusiasm, Christian ardour for certain humane truths, sermons, pieties, schemes, or interests consecrated by the touch of Christ and the atmosphere of the New Testament. It does not realize the gulf that divides such religion from effectual faith and positive godliness. It has not the moral note sufficiently dominant—as the moral note sounds in the Gospel. It is too subjective, and subjectivism invariably leads through sentiment to decadence, and through decadence to public feebleness. Our religious sentiment robs us of spiritual power. That loss robs us of moral strength. And that lack again deprives us of social insight and public weight. The politics of pity destroys the politics of real power. Much of the religion which is most in evidence is a mixture of sentiment and strenuousness. But no amount of strenuousness will keep from decadence sentiment which is without an authoritative moral core. Moral earnestness is not enough. Earnestness of ethical enthusiasm can never do the work of faith in grace. Is strenuousness and sentiment a correct translation of faith which worketh by love? In moving down from grace to love, from holiness to goodness, from justification to righteousness, we fall from the concert pitch of the New Testament. We may have its atmosphere but not its power. We lose the element of evangelical ethic in the atoning cross which keeps sentiment as strong as it is sweet, and as permanent as it is fine. There is no kindness like the moral tenderness of those who are forgiven much.

We are on the threshold of a decadence. We may lose our way and our strength in a warm mist. We may be hypnotized by a vague philosophandering. It is not the Humanism which ignores Christianity that I dread for us. Our peril is the humane piety which is beautifully Christian but think outside the Bible and ignores the distinctive Gospel notes What the detachment from Nature did to debase science and art will be done for our Christianity, unless we recover contact with our source of reality and authority in the Bible Grace. We shall become decadent in our social way, as poetry did in its coffee-house and boulevard way. I have perceived in some of our weaker preachers a certain Christian preciosity, an affectation of the sweet and winning note which had passed into the very manner of speech, and which betrayed sedulous imitation rather than the virile conviction of men who had become themselves in the Gospel.

It is our tendency to think that the way to reach a warm and steady revelation of God is to go deep into the interior of human nature, away from those infinities and sanctities that approach it so coldly from without. And so we say, "Sink into yourself and rise redeemed." Pierce the human and you will find the divine. Penetrate far enough into the human heart and you reach the real presence of a loving God. Make the most of human affection and you arrive at the love of God. Open the heart of a divine man and you will find the heart of a human God. It is an error which I may illustrate by another. It is a popular notion that the warmest part of this island must be in the centre of it, away from the cold waters and high gales of the inconstant sea. But the scientific fact is just the reverse. The sea has a benign and steadying influence upon the climate of the coast. The coldest place in England, according to the charts, is a spot at its very heart. So it is not by retreating into the interior of our humanity or culture that we find the benign and blessed God. The bustle of passion and energy at our human centre can be spiritually colder than where men face the realities that close us in. At the heart of man you will find divine symptoms, but not a divine salvation. *Tendimus in altum.* There is a circumambient grace in the theologies despised by the humanities, a grace that comes to our shore and knocks, yea beats, and even lashes, there; and it has more of the changeless love of God in it than all the affections that sweeten the inlands of life or the culture that adorns it. Sea and shore indeed meet in storm. But our peace lies through storm. Our state is such that our salvation is where God and man meet in a historic crisis, where God's passion to reach us falls upon man's rockbound will not to be found. Herein is love, not that we love, but that God loves and makes awful propitiation for us—

"The best of what we do and are,
Just God, forgive."

XVIII

One sign and source of our religious decadence is the non-ethical disjunction of the Christian life from fear, repentance, forgiveness, and its constant humiliation—in theological language, the detachment of sanctification from justification and regeneration. The word justification has long gone out of our religious vocabulary, and I do not wish to force it back. It will return when the thing returns and demands a name. Its loss is being followed by the word sanctification. And in place of sanctification we find another word and the appeal for another thing—consecration. We must sympathize with much that this implies. But do we remember when we ask people to consecrate themselves to God, that it was the spotless, flawless things that were thus devoted in the Bible? Self-consecration, without more ado, means that we think ourselves worth a holy God's having as we stand. But do the great lives that we call consecrated think that way about themselves? Are they not more occupied with their self-humiliation to God's mercy than their self-consecration to His service? Consecrated service is not the first thing. There are forgiven souls in course of sanctification whom God will not allow to serve Him yet—as Moses might not enter the Promised Land, or David build a house of God. It is part of their punishment. Again, did Paul consecrate himself to his work? He obeyed a call which not only humiliated him, but shattered him. And he found his sanctification in the pursuit of his ministry. Sanctification does not come, as self-consecration is sometimes understood, by working at it, by the culture of holiness as a vocation, but by passing deeper and deeper in self-forgetfulness into the grace, cross, and service of Christ. We do not sanctify ourselves. We had better not know how sanctified we are. The humility which knows how humble it is has ceased to be humble, and so with holiness. We are sanctified by the Holy Ghost while on our Saviour's business. Soul-culture, indeed, we have not enough of, but soul-culture as the pursuit of life is monastic. It grieves and quenches the Spirit to take up holiness as a career. We shall never (I have said above) be holy or real by trying to be either, but only by trusting and loving Him who is both. Self-consecration is but too apt to become self-consciousness. It is not a New Testament word. We should be careful in the use of it, and test it by New Testament ideas. Is it the great New Testament type of faith that prevails in some circles where there is much speech of self-consecration? Is it not more feminine than apostolic, the fruit of pure minds rather than regenerate? Some forms of self-consecration are but sanctification become decadent through detachment from justification by forgiving grace.

The error that constantly besets experimental Christianity (even when it would be repudiated as a doctrine), is that of treating the mission of the Spirit as a new dispensation transcending the work of Christ, and proceeding in some independence of the Bible, going round it instead of through it and its intelligent use. You will find no more childish treatment of the Bible than among some of the circles that are voluble of the Spirit. We keep asking for new pentecosts without going back to the old agony, and the old Calvary, and the Spirit's fontal achievements upon the world powers there. As if Christ sent some influence supplementary to His person and His work which would sanctify us without our immersion in their moral victory and spiritual effect. The spirit that makes Christianity was given once for all in the Christ of history. It was by the Eternal Spirit He offered Himself to God and finished the work given Him to do. The other paraclete could do no other work. Sanctification is but a maturer faith in our justification and a deeper life in our Justifier. It is the growing appropriation of redemption in the Redeemer. There is no way of consecrating one's self or one's Church but by a deeper immersion in the grace of the cross, and by a deeper and more earnest occupation with the Gospel on the great scale. Prayer itself becomes trivial and fruitless, and may mislead us, if it is detached from serious and intelligent use of the Bible.

But you say, perhaps, that the call to consecration is directed to the young—the hopeful, joyful young, who have not yet done or felt serious sin, and cannot be expected to know the humiliation of its forgiveness. But that is the answer of a decadent, subjective individualism. What really makes the penitence and sanctification of the Gospel is not the effect of my sin on me, but the effect of human sin on Christ. We only learn the Christian measure of our sin when we see what the sin of our sinful race means for Christ. Gazing thus our sin we see. If I am not yet stung by sin of mine, at least the Gospel I profess turns on His piercing by the human sin I share. We may speak of the consecration of one who knows no sin, of the self-consecration of Christ, who never felt Himself unworthy to be a sacrifice to God. But we—we are not worthy to consecrate ourselves to God till we are consecrated by God in Christ. We are not worthy to sacrifice ourselves to God if we are not either perfectly holy, or of a broken and contrite spirit, which last is the true sacrifice in the presence of the Atoning Sacrifice and its Grace.

Put Christ before young and old. Let Him consecrate as He will—a Christ really studied out of the New Testament. Let the Gospel do the sanctifying. It is not of man or the will of man. We are in danger of brow-beating and conjuring with the Spirit if we try. He moveth as He will. He is at no man's command, except as we may command by our prayer the grace of God already given in Christ's Cross.

XIX

Our first business is neither to gather men nor to move them, but to preach in the speech of our time (but not its slang) the universal and moving Gospel. Let *it* gather them, and let *it* stir them. The first condition of a true revival is a sound

Gospel. To revive the Church, revive its Gospel as given once for all in its Bible. To reform the Church, reform its Gospel. It is a mischievous notion that any idea of God or Gospel is to be welcomed and supported if only it affect men and "do good." Some people reconcile themselves in this way to movements whose doctrines they have far outgrown, whose methods repel them, and whose temper revolts them. It is a wrong principle. It might justify all kinds of histrionics. If we adopt it, if we admit that any Gospel is good which influences numbers in a wide, rapid, and striking way, we have no case against either Romanism or Buddhism. Both faiths are more successful with human nature than our own —partly because they are more lenient to it. It is the religion that is severest on human nature that has done most for it. It is to that self-searching Gospel, trusted in our charge, that our first fidelity is due. And regeneration by the Gospel on any searching scale depends now on the searching regeneration of much that is offered as Gospel. It needs to be detached from much formal lumber. It needs to be infused with a humaner passion of God's grace, a more ethical grasp of His holiness, and a severer tenderness of His love. It needs to be set free from thorny questions stirred by the Bible as a book, and irrelevant importations from the philosophies. We must clear and lighten the Gospel for action. We must scrape off the barnacles that reduce its speed. We must not fear modern construction or modern tactics. We need all this done in an informed and competent way. We need the kind of theology which is thorough enough to rescue the theology of the Gospel from that of the schools and from that of the street. Theology alone can do it; and it needs much theology to do it. The popular repudiation of theology in the name of Christianity is an offence to the Gospel as well as to intelligence. It is sometimes a refuge of despair, sometimes a device of lazy ignorance. I have mostly found that those who threw about insults to theology were the victims of a bad and amateur theology. They were untrained for their apostolic work. They had not lodged at the Interpreter's House. They did not know their sacred business.

Every truly Christian mind must have a theology. But let us discourage amateurism on these momentous themes. (And no man is an amateur who really knows his Bible well, and better than he knows his age.) Let us aim at something trained and competent—something which is evolved from the theology of the past, from the splendid tradition of Christian mind, as a living growth, and not torn away from it and then flung rudely in its face. All preaching adequate to the time should long ago have been done with the theology of revolt. The man who stops and scolds there is more than a quarter of a century out of date without knowing it. The world of the competent has gone by him. He is outside the science of his subject. But, indeed, the theology of revolt has in great measure passed away. What we are left with now is a thing in some ways less worthy. It is the theology of fatigue, which is confusion. And it dwells hard by the theology of decadence, which is no theology at all, and but a poor order of religion. It is little that the preacher has to do directly with academic and scholastic theology. He need but know what has been done with it, if only to make him realize its failure. Let him replace it with a living theology. For a theology he must have. But he has tried to make theology living by making it sentimental or aesthetic, affectional or literary or mystic. He has drawn it from the poets rather than the apostles. And we are now paying the penalty in our chaos of conviction. To be living, theology must be moral and experimental—that is to say, evangelical. It must turn on personal interest in a moral Atonement. The corrective of academic and Catholic theology is evangelical and Protestant—the theology that begins and ends in holy grace. This alone is realist theology, relevant to the perennial moral nature of life and its central moral need. The other theologies are conventional, scholastic, or romantic.

Some will laugh (and prove how right I am) when I say that the chief need of the ministry in all the Churches is not earnestness, not religion, not ethical interest, not social sympathies, not heart, not work, but *a theology*, an evangelical theology capable of producing all these things, and of making our students as ardent about their truth as young doctors are about theirs. It would give to their word that one thing lacking to fix the many rich colours they dye it in, and to add the note of authority, lucid conviction, and welcome guidance. We have in many cases too much mystic and incommunicable experience in our religious teachers, and too little moral coercion by an objective note. Their word is very rapt, fine, and bold, but it does not come home as the inevitable word, waited for by a confused, sinful, moral world. I think I may appeal to most preachers whether one of the most disheartening things in their ministry is not the failure in carrying home their own certain experience to *men*—their failure to impress with the authority of their message, as they themselves are impressed —practical men, good, wise men of the world, who live habitually in the moral collisions and relations of will and will, and who are more open to considerations powerfully moral than sweetly devout. How many preachers have had to regret the necessity of sacrificing such people to the elementary needs of the mass of the congregation! Is no Gospel possible which shall do what the minister's personal resources cannot do, and meet both? Has it not once been done? Is a doctrine impossible which shall do it again? I do not say we should always succeed, even with what I here desiderate. But we should succeed much oftener and more hopefully. And we should at least leave a respect for our message, the lack of which is not always concealed by genuine respect for ourselves. It is a humiliating position to be accepted as a good fellow by men who think our Gospel moonshine. We want a grasp of the Gospel not only as the filling of the longing soul, nor the salvation of the sinful soul, but as the supreme achievement of a holy God, the supreme fact of the moral universe, and the supreme authority of a moral humanity. We need to realize in Jesus not the children's Christ nor the women's Christ, nor the saint's Christ, nor the poet's, nor the outcast's only, not the Church's Christ alone, nor the Christ of the proletariat, but also the Christ of the moral universe, of the human conscience—the Christ and grace of the holiness of eternal, atoning God.

XX

So I must bear down on an inevitable note. There is but one means by which the authority of grace (and therefore all moral authority) can be established both for the Church and for society. It is the means God Himself had to take to establish it for the world and for eternity. It is the atoning cross. It is the return of the Churches with new insight to the central note of a Gospel of redemption—namely, to the doctrine of grace as expressed in the Atonement. By the cross is meant nothing less than the Atonement. Without it grace loses meaning, and becomes but pity. Without it morals lose reality, and therefore effect. I seem to trace all that is unsatisfactory in the Churches and their relation to Society to the displacement of this doctrine. Anglicanism slights it one way, we in another. On the one hand, as in Anglicanism, it is displaced from the centre by the doctrine of the Incarnation. Bishop Creighton put his keen finger upon this weak spot. "Harm has been done," he says, "by the prominence given in our day to the doctrine of the Incarnation over the doctrine of the Atonement. It weakens the sense of sin, which is one of the greatest bulwarks against unbelief, and through which we live into a larger world." That is more than shrewd. It has insight. Creighton saw deeper than Westcott. The Incarnation is no basis for universal morals. Only the Atonement is, as the moral act of the universe. And only the Atonement gives the Incarnation its base and its value in any moral and religious sense. Without it, it is but a philosophic theme. The Redeemer must be not simply from God, but of God. Only in our reconciliation do we discover that it is God reconciling in Christ.

On the other hand, as in our own Churches, the Atonement is dislodged from its primacy by a genial synopticism without much doctrine of any kind. You can hear sermons on the Christian philosophy of pain as illustrated by the cross without a word about the Christian gospel of grace established there. Yet without the grace of the Saviour pain is still but bane, even in the cross. It is not that the doctrine is denied. It is only retired on a pension. It is stowed in the hold as not wanted on the voyage. It has been taken so much for granted that it is forgotten, like a respected ancestor in the family portraits. Our people treat it as a theologoumenon instead of the marrow of their Christian life. It is not that our beliefs are untrue, but they are out of focus. And the the result is a moral dullness in the Christian public, a religious vagrancy, a spiritual timidity, for which our warmer sympathies or our ethical instincts form but a poor remedy. I do not mean for a moment that our pulpits should ring again with theological disquisition on this head. But I do mean that the note of it should change, and often totally change, the type of our religion and the spirit of our ethic. Much of our current preaching is non-evangelical. There is a dullness, a slackness, a bewilderment in its climate; and it must become evangelical again in spirit and in truth. There is a great difference between preaching that is suffused with this doctrine and preaching that is not. The scientific discussion of the matter let the minister keep for his study or his fraternal meetings. But the atmosphere of the pulpit will be very different according as this doctrine is the active authority of his own living faith or not. I will not say it is another Gospel—though in some cases that would not be too much to say—but at least it is another type of faith.

And let those in the pew not turn from what I say as if it concerned the preachers alone. It carries the Church and its fortunes. It concerns the whole spirit and manner of Christian faith. It is unconsciously at the root of much lay dissatisfaction with the preacher's word, much complaint about its poverty, much restlessness under his ministry. The old orthodoxies can never again be what they were; but one thing in them draws me and sustains me amidst much that is hopelessly out of date. And it is this, that they had a true eye for what really mattered in Christianity; and especially that they did grapple with the final facts of human nature, the abysses of moral experience, the wickedness of the human heart, and its darling self-will. They closed with ultimates. They did not heal lightly the wound of the people. They did confront the last riddle of the world, the last tragedy of the conscience, the last crisis of the soul. They did not toy with the human curse. They did face spiritual reality. They thought on the scale of deep Eternity. In accepting the theology of the Reformation (which was itself a correction of immemorial Catholic thought), they worked with the themes of an old experience, an ecumenical culture, and the universal soul. They did not set up a standard provincial, sectarian, modern, or literary. They had not arrived at the poetic sermon, the sermon of genial ethic and kindly piety, the social sermon, the literary sermon, the Tennyson sermon, and the Browning, and the Whittier worst of all. I have heard many of them, and I have preached more. Oh, do not tell me, for I know, of the romance of passion, the witchery of beauty, and the stately measure of classic grace. I have lived in that land of milk and honey and generous wine. But a curse is on us that these things cannot lift. God be merciful to us sinners!

It is the grace of Israel we need; for the grace of Greece fails heart, and flesh, and moral will. It is subjective sand when we want objective rock. It does not enable us to keep our feet. We need a hand to lift us by the hair, if need be, and hurt us much in the doing of it, if only it set us on the Rock of Ages. And the old Puritans (now sixpence a volume octavo) at least do that. And they do it because, with a very criticizable theology, they stood at the centre of things with their religion of the moral Atonement, of a free but most costly Gospel. They grasped what makes God the Christian God—not only a free grace but a costly. It is not only the freedom of His grace, but its infinite price to Him that makes God God. "By terrible things in righteousness dost Thou answer us, O God of our salvation." These Puritans did what we are losing the moral art to do. They descended into hell before they rose again. They were merciless to their own souls under the mercy of God. They were less gracious than we are; but they owed more to grace. They spoke as men whom the rock had fallen upon and ground to powder, so that from the dust there should be created a new man to stand on that rock for ever. The great Puritan tradition has become staled with much platform use, but we shall never revive it by galvanizing the Puritan heroism—only by sharing the Puritan humiliation. We leave humiliation behind us as we outgrow the first flush of our conversion. But to regain their power we must revisit the same centre and draw from the same spring. And that centre is the atonement of grace and its daily appropriation. It is the pivot and the palladium of Christianity. It is the permanent thing in the Christian creed—the essential thing. The grace of God has no meaning and no power without it. Without it Christianity is but a temporary religion, an interim religion. The doctrine of grace and the doctrine of the Atonement are identical. So those who are shy of the Atonement speak little of grace and far too much of love. But call the doctrine as you will, it is our moral centre.

The loss of effective contact with this reality would explain all the Church's failure in moral power. The Church indeed loves the cross. It were a libel to say otherwise. But it does not always stand on Calvary with both its feet. It does not gaze into the cross with all its soul as Paul did. It does not place it in practice where he did. Its sanctification is not in daily contact with its root in justification, in forgiveness. It is shy of the cross when it should be familiar. And it is over-familiar with it when it should be filled with holy awe. Our free talk of it in our mission addresses would have more effect if we felt it in our Church worship till we hardly dared to speak of it. We could dispense with much preaching about the cross if we had more from beneath it. Our exhibition of it to the world would be more powerful, even if more reserved, did we but regain it as the dominant tone of our faith and the prime element in our Gospel. If the whole Church preached the grace of the cross for its age as Paul did for his and the Reformers for theirs, it would set up a moral authority in the heart of the world which would settle all national and social questions for a willing people with a godly power. The cross is nothing statutory. Its theology is not forensic. It is the focus of that moral order on which Society must live, and the shrine of that holiness which mankind was redeemed to love, honour, and obey. The power is there, the love is there, the light is there. It is we who are timid, bewildered, and unsure. Get you to the stronghold, ye prisoners of hope!

That Redemption of atoning grace is the true moral note of the Gospel. Yet it is singular, nay, startling, this Gospel is not in the great Creeds; it does not appear in the symbols of the Church till the greater Confessions of the Reformation.

The matter of forgiveness and redemption is not in the Athanasian Creed at all. In the Nicene Creed the remission of sins is mentioned only late and in a passing way; which is explained by its mischievous association with a magical baptism at the unconscious beginning of life. And in the Apostles' Creed it is tucked away into a corner near the end; just as we have come to close our beautiful prayers for everything except mercy with a perfunctory afterthought, "And this we ask (with the forgiveness of our sins) through Jesus Christ our Lord." What wonder that the moral authority of the Church has proved such an unstable thing in the course of history when her ecumenical symbols not only do not start from the real source of authority in Christianity, but scarcely allude to it. I mean, of course, redeeming grace. It was inevitable, if Christianity was to survive, that these archaic symbols, with their tremendous missing of the Christian point, should be replaced by the profound and accurate Evangelical Confessions of the Reformation. There is far too much said, even among ourselves, about the Creeds and their simplicity and the way they keep to the Christian facts. Yes, and all but ignore the one fact on which Christianity rests—the fact of redemption by grace alone through faith. It is the supreme Catholic error. For the soul of an ethical Christianity you must go to the great Evangelical Confessions, which contain the true standard for the interpretation of the Creeds in the interest of the Gospel. And when we treat those magnificent Confessions as old lumber, when we banish from our type of Christianity the centrality of grace and live upon love, when we treat forgiveness as a decorous afterthought, when we think it dreary theology to discuss Redemption or Atonement, we are simply returning to the credal condition of Catholicism. We are falling over into a new Catholicism. We are undoing the Reformation liberty by a sentimental liberalism. For the one work of the Reformation was to restore free Grace, Atonement, and

Redemption to be the centre of the Christian world, the spring of the moral world, and the authority for the free human soul.

XXI

It is the confession of grace we need more than the creed of it. It is little that we should say a creed, but it is everything that a Church should be ready with a confession. And it becomes us far more to confess our Saviour in public than to confess our sins. I wish I had the high and venerable authority which would warrant me in inviting you to follow me in a loud and common confession. If I had, it would be this from our Churches to all men, "God so loved the world that He gave His only begotten Son to be a propitiation for us, that whosoever believeth in Him should not perish but should have everlasting life." It is not a creed, it is not a religion we need, but life by a Redeemer. We need a religion which is not a mode of thought or a mode of feeling, but a life in life, first for our soul and also for our Society. When I read, "He loved me and gave Himself for me," do I trouble (when these words are most powerful and precious with me) about their value for Paul's type of religion, or their bearing on a theory of Atonement? Their Gospel of Atonement leaps out of the book and clasps me. Who shall separate me, with all my wretched schism, from Christ's love? Who shall dislodge me from the security of God's love in Christ? I am secure, not because it is written, but because the writing becomes luminous with the passage through it of the Holy Ghost. The wire glows with the current. I have a measure now for the whole of Scripture in the living word which that phrase carries home to my soul. The whole soul of the Bible looks out through that eye, and searches mine, and settles and stills me with the Grace of God. The Bible has done its great work for me (and for the world), not as a document of history, but as a historic means of grace, as the servant of the Gospel, lame, perhaps, and soiled, showing some signs of age, it may be, but perfectly faithful, competent, and effectual always for God and man. God, Sin, Redemption, Eternal Life—it is all one living, mighty, historic reality. There is no doubt (is there?) of the moral drift of history on the whole, of the moral forces at play, of the moral destiny of the soul, or of our falsehood to it. Still less is there doubt of the historic action of a moral redemption. Is it or is it not the supreme act of the God whose holiness at once makes sin sin, and makes it minister to our Eternal Life? I cannot doubt it when words like those arrest me. If our moral nature is the heart of history, our moral salvation is the heart of God in history, the rock of spiritual reality and the authority for social obedience and triumph.

Or, I read the story of the father who beseeches Christ to heal his son. I hear the answer of the Lord, "I will come down and heal him." "Him!" That means me. The words are life to my distempered soul. I care little for them (when I need them most) as a historic incident of the long past, an element in the discussion of miracles. They do not serve their divinest purpose till they come to me as they came to that father. They come with a promise here and now. I see the heavens open, and the Redeemer at the right hand of God. I hear a great voice from heaven, and these words are the words of the Saviour Himself to me, "I will come down and heal him." And upon them He rises from His eternal throne. He takes His way through a ready lane of angels, archangels, the high heavenly host, and the glorious fellowship of saints. They part at His coming, for they know where He would go. These congenial souls do not keep Him, and these native scenes do not detain Him. But on the wings of that word He moves from the midst of complete obedience, spiritual love, holy intelligence, ceaseless worship, and perfect praise. He is restless amid all that in search of me—me sick, falling, lost, despicable, desperate. He comes, He finds, He heals me on the wings of these words. I do not ask the critics for assurance that the incident took place exactly as recorded. I will talk of that when I am healed. It is a question for those who are trying to frame a biography of Jesus, or discussing the matter of miracles. It has brought to dying me the life of Christ. The Gospel of the cross does not make its crucial appeal to human healthy-mindedness. For me these words are more than historical; they are sacramental. They carry not a historic incident merely, but the historic Gospel. Historically, they were never said to me. I was not in the thought of Jesus when He spoke them; neither was I in His thought upon the cross. But by the witness of the Spirit to my faith they come, as if they were said to no one else. I was in His Gospel. They come to me as they are in God. And I live on them for long. And the Bible is precious for their sake. And I wait by their hope, and in the strength of their life I go many nights and days till I come to another mount of God, and the same Gospel speaks and restores me from another holy hill.

I have found my rock, my reality, my eternal life in my historic Redemption. And what is moral rock, real existence, and spiritual mastery for me is also the authority and charter of the Church, the living power in all history, the moral foundation of Society, and the warrant of an infinite future for the race.

www.ingramcontent.com/pod-product-compliance
Lightning Source LLC
Chambersburg PA
CBHW070506100426
42743CB00010B/1773